Interventions
That Work With
Special
Populations
in Gifted Education

Interventions
That Work With
Special
Populations
in Gifted Education

Ariel Baska and
Joyce VanTassel-Baska, Ed.D.

PRUFROCK PRESS INC.
WACO, TEXAS

Library of Congress Cataloging-in-Publication Data

Names: Baska, Ariel, author. | VanTassel-Baska, Joyce, author.
Title: Interventions that work with special populations in gifted education /
  Ariel Baska and Joyce VanTassel-Baska, Ed.D.
Description: Waco TX : Prufrock Press Inc., [2018] | Includes bibliographical
  references.
Identifiers: LCCN 2018017162| ISBN 9781618217097 (pbk.) | ISBN 9781618217110
  (epub)
Subjects: LCSH: Gifted children--Education--United States. | Learning
  disabled children--Education--United States. | Children with social
  disabilities--Education--United States. | Teacher-student
  relationships--United States.
Classification: LCC LC3993.9 .B37 2018 | DDC 371.95--dc23
LC record available at https://lccn.loc.gov/2018017162

Edited by Stephanie McCauley

Cover design by Raquel Trevino and layout design by Micah Benson

ISBN-13: 978-1-61821-709-7

Printed in the United States of America.

At the time of this book's publication, all facts and figures cited are the most current available. All telephone numbers, addresses, and website URLs are accurate and active. All publications, organizations, websites, and other resources exist as described in the book, and all have been verified. The authors and Prufrock Press Inc. make no warranty or guarantee concerning the information and materials given out by organizations or content found at websites, and we are not responsible for any changes that occur after this book's publication. If you find an error, please contact Prufrock Press Inc.

Prufrock Press Inc.
P.O. Box 8813
Waco, TX 76714-8813
Phone: (800) 998-2208
Fax: (800) 240-0333
http://www.prufrock.com

Table of Contents

Preface

The authors have created this text in reaction to the needs of students who are both gifted and live with circumstances or conditions that contribute to underachievement in school. These students are frequently overlooked for services in gifted programs. Due to the problems of language acquisition, disability, or lack of fiscal and family resources, these students are also overlooked for opportunities to develop talents and skills that would allow them to move forward successfully in school and beyond.

This text consists of three parts to provide a thorough overview of the needs of these special populations. It contains both information on necessary interventions and resources on how to create change within classrooms and schools to benefit these students. Part I focuses on who these students are, using research and practice to define their abilities, as well as providing case studies of students who have been successful in schools. Part II defines interventions that have proven successful with these learners at the school and classroom level, as testified by the case studies and intervention studies conducted with learners with special needs. Part III concludes the book by emphasizing the support structures necessary to help these students in school and beyond, including people in students' lives and the programs and services that surround their learning in school.

The audience for this text includes those who seek to know more about these learners. This text will benefit practitioners who work with special populations, including regular classroom teachers, teachers of the gifted, teachers of English language learners (ELLs), Title I staff, and special education teachers who work with twice-exceptional learners. The administrators who run these special programs would also benefit from using the book, as would the counselors and clinicians who see these students on a daily basis, and parents who are advocates for their children with special needs in the home and school settings.

Introduction

Research on twice-exceptional students, English language learners, and students of poverty (see Angelelli, Enright, & Valdés, 2002; Olszewski-Kubilius & Clarenbach, 2014; Weinfeld, Barnes-Robinson, Jeweler, & Shevitz, 2013) demonstrates that these students are often overlooked for gifted services because of a curriculum that does not play to their strengths. Alternatively, if identified, many of these students with special needs underperform when faced with rigid curriculum structures that require narrowly defined behaviors and responses (VanTassel-Baska, 2010) or skill sets not acquired at earlier ages through opportunities external to school (Burney & Beilke, 2008).

Because of the individual issues that minority, ELL, and twice-exceptional profiles present, it is difficult for these students to be identified for gifted or special education programs, as they are likely to develop compensatory strategies that mask either the disability or the talent (Kirk, Gallagher, & Coleman, 2014). Educators may see a flat profile that blends in with the crowd because a student's giftedness is tempered by a learning disability; at the same time, a student who should be identified for special education services will be denied because his or her giftedness lifts test scores and academic achievement just enough to fall within the "normal" range (Weinfeld et al., 2013). Some researchers have focused on identification techniques that would enhance participation of low-income learners and minority groups (Lakin & Lohman, 2011). Yet patterns of underrepresentation of learners with special needs have persisted in identification practices across the United States (McClain & Pfeiffer, 2012).

As a result, national data indicate that the twice-exceptional population is not systematically identified or properly programmed for (Neihart, 2008). Because of dual exceptionality, these students experience great difficulty in negotiating learning pathways. Research suggests that these students, although gifted, have deficits in learning, attention, and socialization behaviors (Foley Nicpon, Allmon, Sieck, & Stinson, 2011). Researchers have also found that comorbidity is a common problem for these students, suggesting that learning disabilities often pair with Attention Deficit/Hyperactivity Disorder (ADHD), autism spectrum disorders (ASD), depression, anxiety disorders, and various other complicating variables, such as minority status and low income, that can make identification even more challenging (Olszewski-Kubilius & Clarenbach, 2014; Weinfeld et al., 2013).

In respect to students of poverty, Ambrose (2013) noted that they are often underidentified due to hiding in plain sight; they are not perceived to have needs that the regular curriculum cannot meet. Moreover, demographic data from the last several decades suggest that the United States is ignoring the effects of poverty on early development by not allowing young children from poverty to receive educational services that would nurture rather than stunt their development (Hodgkinson, 2007). The number of children from poverty appears to be growing, from 39% in 2008 to 44% in 2014 (Jiang, Ekono, & Skinner, 2016). State data also suggest that achievement continues to lag for students from low-income backgrounds, even for those who are identified as gifted (Plucker, Hardesty, & Burroughs, 2013). However, one state study showed enhanced achievement for students of poverty and African American students who were identified using performance-based assessment protocols and who have received 3 years of intervention in gifted programs (VanTassel-Baska, Feng, & de Brux, 2007). Studying the problem from the vantage point of intergenerational data, Chetty, Hendren, Kline, Saez, and Turner (2014) found limited mobility in the U.S. for groups from poverty, suggesting that resource support for people who live in poverty has not been sufficient to affect upward mobility rates.

The issue of geographic location has always been considered a key feature in talent development. Compared to rural settings, cities provide the context for more stimulation, more chances for meeting intellectual peers, and more access to resources for learning and applying skills to various talent areas. Data also suggest that cities have often been viewed as the contexts for high-level talent development, while rural areas have been viewed as less promising contexts for nurturing achievement and productivity in fields of endeavor (Howley, Howley, & Showalter, 2015; Stambaugh & Wood, 2015), even though poverty is an issue in each type of demographic location.

Other researchers have acknowledged areas of need and developed interventions for students from low-income backgrounds. Beck and McKeown (2007), for example, focused on enhancing vocabulary development through the use of thinking strategies. VanTassel-Baska (2017) with her colleagues at William & Mary designed units of study that elevate thinking for these students in all subject areas. Gavin, Casa, Adelson, Carroll, & Sheffield (2009) designed math materials that focus on authentic problem-solving behaviors to provide greater challenge in the curriculum for these students. Yet often the interventions are not tailored enough to be viable for children who have dual conditions or who are both poor and learning English for the first time, for example.

In 2015, the U.S. Census Bureau reported that at least 350 languages were spoken in U.S. homes (American Community Survey, 2015). A large population of young people live bilingually. These students bring diverse cultural and linguistic backgrounds into the educational arena, but for many of them, the struggle with the language and culture of school feels overwhelming. It is not surprising, then, that ELLs are often ignored for inclusion in gifted programs. Their lack of inclusion relates to teacher perceptions of seemingly insurmountable problems with language acquisition. These students' parents usually face as many or more language barriers, meaning that parents who want to advocate often can't. These parents, then, through no fault of their own, are silent on the issue of their child's educational needs (Angelelli et al., 2002; Arias & Morillo-Campbell, 2008).

In response to these concerns, some curriculum materials have been developed to assist with converting the perceived deficits of language to positive uses in the enhancement of learning in other subject areas, such as science (Bianco & Harris, 2014; Dulong-Langley, 2017; Lee & Buxton, 2013). Enhanced fluency in reading has been demonstrated through the use of differentiated instructional strategies (Reis, McCoach, Little, Muller, & Kaniskan, 2011). Moreover, reviews of promising programs and practices have been published (Briggs, Reis, & Sullivan, 2008). Other work has shown direct benefits from an encouragement of the use of nonverbal cues for both identification and teaching (Goldenberg, 2008).

Several texts also highlight best practices for use with ELLs and other special needs populations, some focusing on successful program models emerging from Javits projects (Adams & Chandler, 2014), and others on the curriculum strategies that work effectively with these students (Aguirre & Hernandez, 2011; Stambaugh & Chandler, 2012). Both Ford (2011) and Worrell (2014) emphasized the role of culture and race in the problems related to appropriate education for gifted learners with special needs, suggesting that educators have a view of these students as deficient rather than as talented. Ford and Kea (2009) addressed these issues in their development of a culturally responsive curriculum rich in cultural role models. They also provided materials to help create contexts in which culturally diverse children can be identified. Ford (2013) provided a framework for dynamic thinking to be used by teachers in working effectively with these students.

Hopefully, stakeholders in the educational process understand that each gifted student, particularly when he or she is from a special population, has a unique set of needs and faces a unique set of challenges. Most research has focused on the particular distinctions and characteristics of these gifted learners with special needs, including their challenges in the classroom, rather than on the fact that it is possible for a gifted student to face poverty, have a learning disability, and try to learn English at the same time. These "triple threat" circumstances affect a fair number of students with special needs, complicating the way educators view their needs and how to address them. In this book's study, students from distinct populations and students with complex profiles that included two or more identifiers described common interventions that best addressed their needs. Taking data from the students, their parents, and teachers, the case studies included in this book reveal specific patterns in development across these populations.

The authors of this book suggest that there is no magic bullet, no single intervention that works with all learners at all stages of development. Rather, this text should be used as a resource to guide practitioners and parents through the various needs and interventions identified to help these learners achieve to their full potential.

The Importance of Intervention

Teachers need this intervention text as they struggle to accommodate different sets of needs in the same student. Giftedness has its own set of challenges, but when it is added to the mix of cultural differences, disabilities, poverty, and language, it is especially challenging. Evidence suggests that even though teachers want to provide for the gifted, they often fail to do so in regular classrooms (Farkas, Duffett, & Loveless, 2008). Special populations are especially vulnerable to a lack of appropriate services. Educators may fail to pay attention to the ability level of such students, crafting accommodations for their disability at too low a level or with too limited a scope. A special needs student from inner city poverty, for example, may benefit from an accommodation that provides greater stimulation and exposure to the cultural context of her city, yet may not receive such an accommodation due to lack of perceived need. Art and music instruction may be beyond the capacity of this student's family to provide, and she has never visited world-class museums available in the city. Such cultural enrichment may spark new interests and desire to achieve new learning on the part of such students.

Because students are labeled based on class, culture, and disability, they may not be seen as gifted. Thus, a text focused specifically on gifted learners with special needs is needed to ensure that accommodations in curriculum and instruction are made, based primarily on learners' abilities, not other factors.

Unfortunately, educators too often focus on identification without adequate attention to a plan for effective intervention. Educators in the field of gifted want to identify more of these students to serve, but they have not considered the unique needs that may require accommodations beyond what current programs provide. Educators may pay too much attention to student deficits in planning an educational program for them, ignoring their strengths, which can be considerable (Baska & VanTassel-Baska, 2016; Ford, 2013). Minority children, for example, may seem to lack readiness for particular skills, based on test results, and so they receive remediation in areas of weakness while their talents remain unaddressed. Or twice-exceptional children may receive programming in their deficit area rather than their talent on the grounds that they need to even their capacity to perform in school subjects. Moreover, when a gifted program is constructed, it tends to focus on one area of the curriculum rather than addressing a whole program of studies. Thus a "program" may be a 2-hour session in project work one day a week. Such fragmentation of services leaves these students without adequate support for accommodations that would enable their talent development.

Using This Text

This text examines the research on these special populations, offers an overview of their needs, focuses on necessary interventions, and provides resources to develop the talents of these students and create change within classrooms and schools.

Part I of this text introduces the target populations of gifted learners with special needs, what is know about them, and the research base on their intervention needs. The authors then present case studies of 10 students, highlighting their strengths and areas for improvement, what interventions worked for them at each level of their school years, and the people in their lives who impacted their development. This section of the book also considers commonalities among the profiles of these students, discussing the overlap of needs and concerns. Talent trajectories are also included, and the section concludes with common misconceptions regarding special populations of gifted learners.

Part II describes interventions that directly respond to the needs identified by the students in this book's research. These interventions represent archetypal activities for use with gifted learners with special needs in differing subject areas and levels of learning. The 10 prototype case studies from Part I directed the inclusion of these approaches. Students not only identified these strategies as the most effective, but they also credited them, in some instances, with their success throughout their years of schooling. Additional interventions are recommended in the area of affective development, based on a literature review of the social and emotional development of gifted learners with special needs. For each intervention, at least two model lessons have been included to illustrate how the strategy might be translated into classroom activities. In addition, teacher tips accompany each strategy, to be used as a guide for best practices with the identified intervention.

Part III centers on the support structures needed to ensure that gifted learners with special needs receive appropriate services in schools, homes, and communities. This section begins by discussing the need for advocacy and includes a guide for all stakeholders in the education process to effect change on behalf of students. This section also discusses beneficial teacher characteristics, as identified in the case studies from Part I, and classroom organization structures that aided those students in their development. The section then shifts focus to the parental role, with suggestions for parents in the home and a discussion for teachers on how to involve parents in the educational process. Part III concludes with implications regarding work with these special populations based on current research, as well as possible areas of future study.

PART I
Who Are Gifted Learners With Special Needs?

When will we also teach them who they are?
We should say to them—
You are unique—you are a marvel
In this whole world there is no one like you and
There never will be again.

—Pablo Casals

It is important to ensure that educators understand who these students are, both in respect to their giftedness and their disability or socioeconomic and linguistic status. Thus, this book begins with clear definitions regarding what the authors mean by twice-exceptionality, students from poverty, and English language learners. Given these conditions, what does giftedness look like in these students? Who are they as individuals?

Defining Special Populations of Gifted Students

Twice-exceptional students are gifted students who are identified with learning, behavioral, or social problems that lead to a dual diagnosis for these conditions and giftedness. Twice-exceptional students may have a number of different underlying conditions that require attention, including autism spectrum disorders (Foley Nicpon, Assouline, Schuler, & Amend, 2010; Gallagher & Gallagher, 2002; Neihart & Poon, 2009), Attention Deficit/Hyperactivity Disorder (Kennedy, Banks, & Grandin, 2011), learning disabilities, and other syndromes that can interfere with learning. These students are most frequently identified first for their disability rather than their giftedness, although sometimes the gifted label emerges in the overall workup and testing of these students.

Gifted students from poverty are those identified as gifted who are on free or reduced lunch. Although poverty may be seen in multiple ways in the larger societal context, educational definitions have centered exclusively on income levels in households. The National Center for Education Statistics (NCES, 2016) has characterized a school as high-poverty when more than 75% of its students are eligible for a free or reduced-price lunch. In 2012–2013, about 24% of students attended public schools that were classified as high-poverty. Using this high-poverty definition enables educators to identify important differences among students: 45% of Black and Hispanic students attended high-poverty schools, compared to 8% of White students. Thus, definitions of poverty are comingled with race. In the 2014–2015 school year, nearly half of Hispanic and Black public school students, one-third of

American Indian/Alaska Native students, and one-quarter of Pacific Islander students attended high-poverty schools. In contrast, 17% of students of two or more races, 15% of Asian students, and 8% of White students attended high-poverty schools. Problems with interventions for these students often are related to teachers not knowing who they are and therefore not being able to target interventions for them as a distinct group.

Gifted ELLs are those who are identified as "gifted and English language learners needing support for language development in English" (National Association for Gifted Children [NAGC], 2011). According to the NCES (2016), Spanish was the home language of 3.7 million ELLs in 2014–2015, representing 77.1% of all ELLs and 7.6% of all public K–12 students. Arabic, Chinese, and Vietnamese were the next most common home languages (spoken by approximately 109,000; 104,000; and 85,300 students, respectively). In 2014–2015, a greater percentage of public school students in lower grades than in upper grades were ELLs. For example, 16.7% of kindergarteners were ELLs, compared to 7.8% of sixth graders and 6.5% of eighth graders. Among 12th graders, only 4.1% of students were ELLs. This pattern is driven, in part, by students who are identified as ELLs when they enter elementary school but obtain English language proficiency before reaching upper grades. The issue of gifted students who are ELLs is most critical at the elementary level, where they may be left out of gifted programs until they reach an appropriate linguistic competency level. Even then, they may not be systematically considered.

Some of these learners may not be readily identified as gifted in a given school district due to the nature of their conditions. Low-income learners often have depressed ability and aptitude scores, based on limited exposure to quality stimulation and early education. English language learners may not be identified as gifted due to language and cultural barriers in schools. Students who are twice-exceptional with a learning disability may not qualify for programs that require high-level functioning in all areas of learning.

Etiology and Comorbid Conditions

Rarely do students experience one learning problem in isolation. Students with specific learning disabilities will often exhibit more than one learning disability in addition to other learning problems, such as ADHD (Berninger & Abbott, 2013; Lyman, Sanders, Abbott, & Berninger, 2017). Students who are twice-exceptional often exhibit a host of symptoms both at home and at school, ranging from learning problems, to depression, to anxiety disorders, to compulsive behaviors, to migraine headaches. These comorbid conditions are fairly typical among students identified as twice-exceptional (Hughes, 2011). At the same time, almost 14% of the ELL population has been identified as having disabilities as well (NCES, 2015). Perhaps this percentage is understandable, given that the language problems and cultural barriers ELLs face may elicit negative behaviors leading more readily to disability identification. Many twice-exceptional students are also on a series of medications to treat different aspects of their problems. Their parents may be proactive in observing their problems and seeking medications that could improve them, along with providing a series of personal interventions that might help. It is also fair to say that successful treatments for these students are short-lived. What works for a student from ages 8–10 no longer does at age 11. Adolescence brings its own set of challenges that may require retuning the interventions and their intensity (Baum, Cooper, & Neu, 2001; Trail, 2011).

Students who are second language learners primarily exhibit problems related to language acquisition. These problems understanding high-level English concepts may hinder these students' ability to communicate to others their higher level thinking abilities. Difficulty understanding concepts also impedes their ability to translate their ideas fluently into written and oral communication (Dulong-Langley, 2017). Often these students remain silent in discussions due to this problem. Sometimes they also have a disability of some kind, which further masks their abilities.

Students who are members of minority groups may be perceived to exhibit the characteristics of their group more strongly than individual characteristics. Consequently, their minority status can prevent them from appearing ready for advanced work. Educators may see these students as reflecting group stereotypes without fully recognizing their abilities. In one study (VanTassel-Baska, 2010), students from different minority backgrounds preferred using different modes of expression to communicate learning. African Americans were likely to enjoy the expressive arts as a mode of talent display, often using nonverbal approaches to convey their ideas in music, dance, and the visual arts. Hispanic students were similar in that regard, perhaps due to language issues. Asian students also preferred nonverbal media to present their abilities, often in math and science-related areas. Students of poverty demonstrated characteristics similar to those of their cultural groups. White students of poverty modeled their behavior more closely on their higher socioeconomic White peers, using social cues and language to emulate their peers.

The central learning characteristics possessed by gifted minority students and students from poverty typically include:

1. openness to experience,
2. nonconformity and independent thinking,

3. creative and fluent thinking,
4. preference for oral expression,
5. quickness to blend feelings with thoughts,
6. responsiveness to multiple modes of learning as displayed in the arts,
7. preference for hands-on applications,
8. preference for real-world connections, and
9. responsiveness to individual learning patterns (VanTassel-Baska & Stambaugh, 2007).

A curriculum that is responsive to such learners will need to possess enough flexibility to address these characterological needs. A multipronged approach to both curriculum and instruction is necessary to address these students' needs and those of the other populations of interest in this book.

Case Studies of Successful Students From Special Populations

In order to support the ideas presented in Part II of the book, the authors collected data on students who represent the special needs characterized in Part I of this book, providing brief vignettes of the students as learners on the journey to talent actualization. The 10 vignettes presented were constructed through the use of multiple data sources in order to enhance their credibility and provide a more complete view of the students as learners.

Methodology

In constructing these student profiles, the authors collected data from three distinctive sources: (1) written documentation on student behavior and performance, (2) surveys and interviews with parents and students, and (3) observations in the classroom context. The authors began by evaluating each student's Individualized Education Plan (IEP) and 504 plan. After incorporating the knowledge gleaned from school documents into practice, they evaluated the plans' efficacy, documenting what did and did not work best for each student. They also interviewed the students, their counselors, and their parents using a common set of questions. One researcher carefully observed students' behavior in Latin classes, in respect to their approaches to learning. Data were compiled across at least 3 years of such observations, providing longitudinal portraits of students' behaviors and learning patterns. All of the students in the study have now graduated from high school; some of them have graduated from college. Each of them, regardless of current schooling level, reflected on all levels of the schooling enterprise. The methodologies employed were a combination of survey questionnaires, where students recorded some information on schooling issues, and interview data collected more informally. All students were 16–18 when they completed the questionnaires. Parents also completed questionnaires. All data were analyzed qualitatively, using a content analysis model to find themes that best represented the commentary collected (Creswell & Creswell, 2018).

Max

Max is a male student from a low-income family, who was also diagnosed with ADD (attention deficit disorder)[1], emotional disturbance, and dysgraphia. He was not identified as gifted despite showing high ability in verbal areas from an early age. From teacher observations across his middle and high school years, Max appeared to be a generally happy student, who vacillated between extreme excitement and boredom and/or fatigue. He could be very charming, vocal, and attentive when engaged, but often retreated into books when exposed to the same or similar material for more than 10 minutes. He also seemed fatigued on a daily basis and usually nodded off at least once every day in class, but with the focused attention of the teacher and specific direction, he seemed to come alive. He was a highly verbal student who excelled in presentations and classroom discussions, but he couldn't express his thoughts in writing easily, due to his dysgraphia and poor organizational skills. His parents did not feel that they could adequately explain Max's academic difficulties. They theorized that he was a "bored gifted student with a possible mood disorder." Max said of himself at the time, "I know I'm smart, but I only realize that outside of school, when I'm making connections to the real world. School is so far from reality . . . I can't play the game [of school]."

Because Max often did not pay attention to the details of what he read, he required test directions to be read to him or instructions given to him. In other settings, his reading and writing needed to be structured with graphic organizers. Max tended to become overwhelmed by assignments and spent time thinking about tangential topics rather than focusing his thoughts on the topic at hand. He needed a clear road map or table of contents to help him in reading English passages or outlining his thoughts when he needed to write.

Ideally, Max would have had a computer on hand at all times to help him take notes, because he could type much faster than he could write with a paper and pen. Unfortunately, given his history of losing school-supplied electronic note-taking devices, the school district would no longer provide him with one, nor were his parents able to purchase one. As a result, a teacher provided him with a small recording device that he wore around his neck to

---

1   *Note.* ADD was the terminology used when this student was identified. The Diagnostic and Statistical Manual of Mental Disorders, Third Edition, Revised (DSM-III-R; American Psychiatric Association, 1987) was the first to introduce the term Attention Deficit/Hyperactivity Disorder (ADHD), eliminating the Attention Deficit Disorder (ADD) diagnosis. The DSM-IV (APA, 1994) and the subsequent revisions through the current DSM-V (APA, 2013) have included three subtypes of ADHD (predominately inattentive, predominately hyperactive/impulsive, and combined).

record lectures and class discussions for future reference. Max also needed further opportunities for metacognition to help him think about his own thinking process. He became deeply engaged in conversations about how he thought and learned best, and wanted to test his own hypotheses. He needed to be aware of himself on this level and spend time evaluating his own learning.

Like many gifted students, Max suffered from chronic boredom in many of his classes. He felt uninterested in doing busywork. He admitted that sometimes he took pride in not listening and still being able to understand the material, although he also admitted that as classes became more difficult in middle school and high school, that particular pride all but disappeared.

His family provided a different view of Max, one of a boy who exhibited few problems at home:

> [W]e tried to be as supportive as possible with Max but had limited time to spend with our two children each night on homework. We do not feel that we can adequately explain Max's problems in school. The bright boy we know at home has always had trouble fitting in at school.

Max, however, took his learning at school very seriously. He worked on developing his strongest skills and abilities through acting and presenting when possible. He needed to be able to use his strengths to access new information. He desperately needed to know that he was developing and growing, a key to his self-concept.

His teachers used the following approaches to help Max develop self-knowledge: (1) preassessments that allowed Max to consider what he already knew on a topic and discuss how he would like to learn more, (2) exit tickets/surveys regarding what confused him about a reading, and (3) postassessment surveys (*What did I do to study that worked? What didn't work for me?*). Max also benefited from using sticky notes to write down study questions and identify themes while working on papers and reading articles, as well as discussing how to know when he was done with a piece of writing.

Max, however, was clearly aware of his difficulties with writing. He commented to an interviewer, "I have books in my mind, chapters in my elbow, and my fingers leak out one bloody word at a time." This quote alone is very telling, as it reveals Max's awareness of his cognitive problems, his intellectual ability to create a graphic metaphor for his experience of writing, and his emotional response to it.

After high school, Max entered a local community college and earned his associate's degree. He currently works in computer and phone repairs but regrets that a bachelor's degree is out of reach for him financially at this time.

Laura

Laura is a female student who was born deaf and uses American Sign Language (ASL) as her first language. Laura was fully mainstreamed in the public school setting, accessing all of her classes with the aid of interpreters who translated for her in the classroom. She had excellent work habits in all of her classes except for math, which was her weakest subject area. She was an avid reader who read many college-level texts in middle school and expressed herself well, both orally and in writing. Despite her verbal abilities, she was not identified as gifted. She also came from a low-income family that could not afford to send her to college. Thus, procuring college scholarships was an important consideration for her.

Although Laura was a student who regularly shone in class, she had difficulty accessing some areas of the curriculum due to her disability, and sometimes shut down, either by retreating into a book or, at times, becoming defiant. She responded well to stories about people, facts, and details, and translated literature at a higher level than most of her peers, but she often had difficulty understanding the finer points of grammar and would disengage from the material at hand if it was not represented visually.

In Latin, she experienced difficulty relating to the "sonics" of poetry, such as meter and figures of speech. At one point, she insisted that she could not be expected to learn how to scan poetry due to her disability—that she simply couldn't scan, no matter what. *Scansion* refers to how many short versus long vowels there are in a line of poetry, which affects how it is read aloud. It can also affect interpretations of the grammar and, therefore, how a line can be translated. Because scansion is in the program of studies and on the Advanced Placement (AP) exam for Latin, Laura could not be excused from this material. Because she couldn't hear the vowel sounds, she didn't believe she could evaluate them, but by working individually with her teacher and a like-minded interpreter, and receiving a list of rules about how to tell a long vowel from a short one, she was able to learn scansion even better than her hearing peers.

This experience taught Laura and her teacher that she could learn anything, and learn it well, as long as she was provided a list of procedures to follow in a step-by step process. She needed the structure and visual confirmation of the rules for both scansion and other grammar points. Using a "formula" was important for her, despite her weakness in math.

As with any deaf student, graphic organizers and organized notes were important accommodations because they allowed Laura to process the material in structured ways. She also benefited from use of the SmartBoard, as it allowed both the teacher and students to mark up the text studied at any given time, so that she could see the discussion unraveling on the board, not just through her interpreter's hands.

Laura suffered from chronic boredom with school due to her intellectual ability, which set her apart from her peers, and she had difficulty communicating with others. To succeed, she needed teachers who structured conversation in class through a Socratic seminar or other means and engaged with her in discussion, making connections with any of her various intellectual interests.

She also required guidance regarding her future career path. She said:

> I don't have definite plans for the future when it comes to jobs, but perhaps I'll be a history researcher, translator of works written in foreign tongues, or a scholar in classical history or languages, such as Hebrew, Latin, or Greek.

Laura completed 5 years of Latin while concurrently enrolled in Spanish for two of those years. She attended the prestigious Virginia Governor's Latin Academy during the summer after her junior year, with the aid of interpreters. Latin Academy was a residential experience, allowing her to take college-level classes over a 3-week period. She was the first deaf student to attend a Governor's School Language Academy in the state of Virginia. She also won numerous awards related to her study of Latin, from gold medals on the National Latin Exam, to scholarships offered by the National Junior Classical League. She described her time in the Latin program by saying:

> Truly, the period which I spent in the Latin program . . . was a time of great intellectual flourishing in my life . . . [Latin] class was always the eye of the storm, so to speak, in the barren desert of my formal education . . . Indeed, my time in the Latin program cast a luster on that part of my life, which had been utterly shorn of meaningful accomplishments . . .

After graduation, with the help of her Latin teacher and a career and transition counselor at her school, Laura obtained a full scholarship to a selective in-state school. She has obtained assistantships during the summers to work more closely with her professors on research projects. She plans to graduate early with a bachelor's degree in Greek and pursue her doctorate in the field.

Ryan

Ryan is a male student, diagnosed with ASD, emotional disturbance, and dysgraphia, but he was never identified as gifted during his years in school. He was always eager to share his knowledge and participate in class in any way that he could. He was highly motivated in his classes, but when frustrated, he tended to react very strongly. He sometimes raised his voice or used inappropriate tone or language in reaction to certain triggers. He had been a victim of bullying in the past and was very concerned with the perceptions of other students. Ryan could become embarrassed easily. He also was very worried about equity in the classroom and would immediately stand up for himself or any other student if he perceived something as unfair.

Ryan suffered from problems with organization and motor coordination, particularly in respect to writing. He often had difficulties finding homework or notes if they had been handwritten, and he would become frustrated looking for things in his backpack or binder, which could be a trigger for him. Ryan also became frustrated when teachers didn't recognize his talents, either because of his difficulties with handwriting or social communication. He excelled in his scientific knowledge of various species and brought outstanding vocabulary skills to the classroom, in addition to many interesting scientific connections. Ryan was deeply focused on a few subjects that were of interest to him. He talked a lot about certain characters from teen fiction and comic books that appealed to him, but he was most passionate about animals.

As for many students with disabilities, the use of a laptop was crucial for Ryan. The laptop allowed him to save assignments, e-mail his homework and classwork, and access helpful applications and websites that extended his knowledge on certain topics. The laptop also allowed him to learn a new way of thinking about file organization, and he began scanning and saving important papers as PDFs on his computer.

Ryan required a significant amount of teacher direction to stay on task if other students in the room were talking, as they were a significant source of distraction for him. However, at the same time, he could not bear to complete work in the hallway or in the neighboring computer lab, as that separated him from peers. This caused his teachers considerable frustration until they realized that he needed to learn to organize his thoughts, his time, and his work in highly structured ways as a part of a regular routine. By asking him to work on a separate graphic organizer, which indicated how much time he had to complete an assignment and specific time requirements for each section, teachers found that Ryan was much less distracted by other people, as his work became a race against the clock. Helping him to organize his binder and his backpack aided his concentration as well.

One of his teachers consulted with Temple Grandin, a well-known advocate for autism spectrum disorders, about Ryan. Grandin used her own experiences and her passionate interest in animals to provide clear-cut advice: Provide Ryan with as much career guidance as possible and make sure he is counseled with directions that will help him become a strong candidate for jobs. As a result of the teacher taking that advice to heart, Ryan visited the career services center at school once a month during his junior and senior years, doing research on what careers might be appropriate for him and familiarizing himself with the requirements. Ryan commented on the role of teachers in assisting him in high school:

> I always appreciated when teachers tried to help me as a person, not just a student. Latin certainly helped me with writing, with scientific names, but my Latin teacher was the first to help me figure out how to get an interview or an internship or pursue zoology as a major in college.

Ryan completed his third year of Latin during his senior year, which he hoped would further his knowledge in working with animals on a scientific level. After graduation, he attended a local 4-year university, which enabled him to live at home and commute for classes. He is currently pursuing a degree in marine biology and maintains a wide circle of friends.

Andrea

Andrea is a female student, diagnosed with learning disabilities, ADD[2], and depression, who was not perceived to be in need of special education services until high school, when she received a 504 plan for processing difficulties. She also had physical problems with both hearing and vision from birth. She was identified as gifted in third grade, showing verbal abilities in the form of winning fourth place in the regional spelling bee and doing book projects at a high school level.

Andrea was a quick learner and often did independent work to advance her studies. She revealed her strengths and interests in verbal puzzles and games but disliked discussions, preferring to read rather than engage in classroom activities. She had many problems with task completion, particularly with homework, but always performed well on tests and quizzes. Allowing her to work independently during discussion proved essential to her optimal performance in class. Teachers noted that she disengaged from class during group work as well, although her performance on assessments and essays was stronger than teachers would have expected.

Andrea believed the most successful interventions were those involving acceleration and independent learning:

> I did best in circumstances where teachers gave me support structures and permission to delve deeper into topics on my own at my own pace. I always felt most engaged and successful in school when I could take advanced coursework. Studying subjects in the 3-week talent search model made me realize my own abilities and encouraged me to continue reading and writing in greater depth.

Because of these interventions, Andrea was able to accelerate her learning by receiving credit for her summer work in talent search programs, as well as AP credit. She also was able to take college courses at her local university and graduate one semester early.

According to her parents, Andrea showed early signs of verbal giftedness. They noted, "Andrea had an early interest in materials related to books and

---

2   *Note.* ADD was the terminology used when this student was identified. The Diagnostic and Statistical Manual of Mental Disorders, Third Edition, Revised (DSM-III-R; American Psychiatric Association, 1987) was the first to introduce the term Attention Deficit/Hyperactivity Disorder (ADHD), eliminating the Attention Deficit Disorder (ADD) diagnosis. The DSM-IV (APA, 1994) and the subsequent revisions through the current DSM-V (APA, 2013) have included three subtypes of ADHD (predominately inattentive, predominately hyperactive/impulsive, and combined).

reading, often picking them up and pretending to read. She also loved to dance and perform for others." At the elementary level, she participated in gifted enrichment Saturday and summer programs at two local universities outside of school.

She described the accommodations during the elementary and middle school years as minimal, with a weekly 45-minute pull-out experience. Acceleration in foreign language coursework and participation in a nongraded drama group that included students from grades 7–12 promoted her interest and accelerated her skill development during these years.

The need for a math tutorial became apparent when Andrea began taking Algebra I as an eighth grader. At that time, Andrea faced problems with math at the high school level as it became more complicated and difficult for her, but she had a math teacher who worked with her intensively after school and helped her to learn. She experienced a lack of school flexibility regarding what courses she could take at one school she attended, which she said had "a narrow view of education and a disdain for students with atypical problems and learning needs."

Interventions that did not work for Andrea were those that focused on remediation in areas of weakness, such as math:

> Most teachers in math focused on repetitious remediation, rather than trying new things with me. Because of my visual problems that went unrecognized, teachers became frustrated with the fact that I wasn't learning in spite of the many math problems placed in front of me. It was only a tutor outside of school who helped me to learn math concepts and to recognize my visual difficulties so I could work around them.

Teachers also gave Andrea difficulty, especially those who emphasized procedure over content and took points off for appearance in written and oral work. She also butted heads with teachers who forced cooperative group learning as the only mode of learning in the classroom.

Despite her problems, Andrea received many awards and honors in school. She was a Commended Scholar in the National Merit Program and an AP Scholar by junior year. She received awards for her performance on the National Latin Exam for 5 consecutive years, receiving a perfect score one year. She was one of 43 students selected statewide to participate in the Governor's School Latin Academy. At Latin Academy, she was the lead in a play performed entirely in Latin.

After taking 5 years of Latin, Andrea graduated from high school one semester early. She attended a selective 4-year university, graduated with a degree in Classics, and is pursuing a career in teaching.

Mitch

Mitch is an Asian male English language learner who came from a low-income family and was formally identified as gifted in sixth grade. He was diagnosed with ASD and emotional disturbance due to his selective mutism. He was an excellent writer with outstanding verbal skills that put him far above his peers in respect to his use of vocabulary, critical thinking skills, and maturity of thought. Mitch typically completed all assignments and assessments with the top grade in the class. Yet Mitch was very reluctant to speak, even in situations where he had much to say on a topic, due to social anxiety. When he did speak, he did so very quietly and was often misinterpreted. Many teachers underestimated his skills, based on his problems with communication. Sometimes his problems were comingled in teachers' minds with English not being his native language.

Although his peers respected his skills and talents, he had few friendships at school. His older peers from Latin class and Latin club were his social network at school, after school, and at extracurricular competitions. His mother believed very strongly that Latin helped him to grow in his social development. Mitch was very interested in social issues and could make excellent arguments for his stances. He felt very strongly that he would like to work for a nonprofit organization.

One of the more important accommodations for Mitch was allowing him to work independently. He often shut down in group-work situations as soon as he had completed his part of the task. At first, teachers suspected that this was due to his social anxiety. However, further inquiry revealed that he didn't feel challenged doing only one component of a project as a part of a group. He preferred being able to delve into all aspects independently. He also needed (on occasion) to give presentations to his teachers after school or present information in a less stressful format than an oral presentation for the whole class.

His perception of the effectiveness of teachers and others in the school context was mixed. He commented:

> Personal interventions of teachers to accelerate content have helped develop learning skills and increased initiative in self-teaching and interest in content learned. Interventions by school social workers and other support personnel involved in my IEP plan have had no effect.

He further commented:

> Discontinued therapy sessions in high school have led to a sense of distrust of official school or professional resources, such as disability accommodations, and aversion to seeking professional help for psychological issues and related educational issues, but the learned impression that I am as well-equipped to apply psychological or clinical knowledge and principles to myself as a professional (less trust in the professional/institution as a "subject supposed to know" in Lacanian terms) has led to increased initiative in seeking solutions and "self-treatment" techniques (such as practice regulating breathing and other physiological symptoms of anxiety that increase anxiety).

This quote illustrates the difficulties Mitch faced working with clinical professionals in school, but also his determination to find out more about himself. His self-regulatory techniques helped him work through his emotional disturbance and improved his performance in school overall. Mitch was proud of this level of self-awareness. In the academic setting, Mitch was proudest of his independent self-designed poetry translation project in 11th-grade Latin class. Consistent with this higher level work, he found special accommodation for his abilities when selected for the summer experience of a Governor's School:

> My participation in a Governor's Latin Academy program, which included intensive learning in Latin and Greek, helped me to be more comfortable with learning foreign languages such as Russian and German at a slightly accelerated pace (12- and 8-week classes covering a semester worth of content), as well as with learning quickly in other subjects, partly due to developing familiarity with learning skills and partly due to developing familiarity with typical expectations in an academic setting (e.g., being able to gauge what and how much I would be expected to study for a quiz based on one textbook chapter).

He still uses compensation strategies in the form of listening to music, looking at work from a variety of different angles to connect with the material, and seeking help from peers.

Over the years, acceleration was the most important accommodation for Mitch. His teacher commented:

> In Latin II, he began work on advanced Latin III material and was able to pass the Latin III final exam with flying colors.

At his request (and after a little teacher investigation), Mitch skipped Latin III and jumped into AP Latin as a sophomore. His mother felt that the acceleration may have made it more difficult for him to make friends in class, but I argued that he needed to be with his intellectual peers, engaged with higher level material. He scored a 5 on the AP exam, the highest score possible, demonstrating that he was more than ready to engage in the advanced level of study mapped out for him.

In regard to acceleration, Mitch noted:

> I believe acceleration of content throughout my K–12 education has given me the preparation to take advantage of opportunities more suited to me after high school (such as accelerated progress in Latin classes giving me opportunities for college Latin courses more appropriate to my level of knowledge) as well as put me ahead of my peers in terms of general academic skills and comfort with learning pace in community college.

Mitch enrolled in a sixth year of Latin, an independent study course designed especially for him. All throughout high school, he participated in Certamen, a statewide Latin quiz bowl held each month of the academic year. He also earned perfect scores on every National Latin Exam and won various awards from the National Junior Classical League. Of Mitch's work with the Latin program, his mother wrote the following:

> I am most grateful for the transformation that I have seen in my son, in terms of his participation in Certamen . . . [which he kept as] his top priority . . . for the last 3 years, which in itself is nothing short of miracle, considering how limited his social world has been all of his school life since first grade; his coming out of the comfort zone to be in these team competitions has been possible only through the deep trust that the teacher has built within him. No therapists or counselors have ever been able to help him take such [a] risk to be out in public eye on a regular basis.

His mother continued:

> Since my child is a very private person with overwhelming social anxiety disorder, the two times that I can say he truly flourished were when he had opportunities to explore his inner aptitude and abilities as a writer in seventh-grade English and a language lover in all 5 years of Latin from grades 8–12. His love of writing and literature was very carefully cultivated

by his seventh-grade English teacher, who gave him the time and attention to grow; his love of the language in general expanded to the genuine curiosity in translation of the classical language under the meticulous and gentle guidance of the Latin teacher, who nurtured him at every level of his language acquisition. In fact, these two areas of interest—writing and translation of classical languages—have ultimately become his career interest.

His mother reflected on the positive aspects of her son's experiences throughout school:

My child may probably be one of the students who, despite their emotional/social issues (he was diagnosed with selective mutism and social phobia), still show the hope of resilience and achievement as long as there is at least one adult (two teachers in his case) who may be willing to invest time, care, and energy in nurturing whatever might seem to be the potential area of growth in the child.

After Mitch graduated, he went to a local community college but received scholarships to transfer to a selective college. He plans to continue his study of linguistics.

Carla

Carla is a female student, identified as gifted with a learning disability (nonverbal) and diagnosed with an unspecified attention disorder, depression, anxiety disorders, and emotional disturbance. She has strong linguistic abilities, which showed in her engagement with Latin over 5 years. She was always a standout student for her ability to connect grammar concepts to a larger understanding of the figurative language of specific authors. At the same time, she taught herself ancient Greek and, on her own initiative, started a Greek club, where she taught other students the same material. Her artistic predispositions led her to take AP Studio Art, which provided a context for addressing her visual-spatial weaknesses.

Carla was identified as gifted at age 8 in second grade. Peer interactions, as well the observations of parents, adults, and teachers, led her to believe she was gifted. Learning problems did not emerge until age 13 in eighth grade, based on test information. Her anxiety and problems with visualization were the primary areas of concern in her functioning well at early stages of her schooling.

She noted her strengths and strategies for compensation:

> I am verbally gifted, and I often have to verbalize my thought process or change the way I am thinking of something that is more visual into a conceptual or word-based format. Also, I have been practicing areas of weakness diligently, allowing myself to recognize weakness but not accept that as the end-all-be-all in terms of study and personal growth. For example, I am challenged in terms of visualization and spatial understanding, so I take classes, such as painting and advanced math and physics, that allow me to work with, not against, the underdeveloped parts of my brain. I find that in doing that, I gain a lot of confidence and am more able to work with my brain as a whole, rather than compartmentalizing subjects into "things I'm good at" and "things I can't do."

Carla experienced only one gifted pull-out class period once a week from ages 9–12, which did not provide the support she needed from those teachers, who saw her weaknesses, not her giftedness, in those project-based programs. For her disabilities, she received physical therapy for lack of fine motor skills and benefited especially from fine motor therapy. According to Carla, this therapy "helped me learn to write, and I would not be the same without it; cognitive therapy also helped me manage my emotional disabilities."

Teachers who were supportive were those who provided adaptations to Carla's learning environment and provided encouragement for her to perform at her highest level. She noted:

> [T]eachers who understand that I am often much more successful when I am in control of my environment and can leave or make myself more comfortable in it have helped me a great deal. I also recognize that emotional understanding and support from teachers has helped me come to terms with myself.

Carla appeared to benefit the most at all levels from interventions that were personalized and provided frequent teacher direction. She also enjoyed group discussion, question-asking, and one-on-one conversations with peers and teachers. Graphic organizers were a boon to her instructionally, as was the flexible use of time some teachers permitted for her. She commented on the teaching techniques she found most effective:

> Frequent direction and personal relationships with teachers . . . helped me, as well as many other techniques that I did not receive until high school, because I was not diagnosed as disabled until then, and even so, my giftedness makes any disability I have almost invisible, and my disability often makes any giftedness I have seem lesser. Because of this, not many teachers tried to help me or create a better learning environment for me, for it seemed I didn't need it.

Carla received little individualized attention or instruction for her disabilities from most teachers, partially because of a late diagnosis in her teenage years. Because of her reticence to seek attention, she was not a strong self-advocate either, instead using self-reflection as a means to understand what was happening in her learning. In respect to receiving so little intervention for her abilities, Carla commented:

> I can only speak of the harm that the lack of intervention has brought, and that is mostly psychological. It took me a very long time to accept my strengths and weaknesses as they are and work past them because I was conditioned to think that I was being difficult or overly sensitive until I was diagnosed.

Despite her disabilities, Carla was quite successful, especially in high school, accruing honors and awards, including individual contest awards, testing awards, honor roll, and acceptance into selective programs such as Governor's School Latin Academy (which she cited as an important experience in her development). She was accepted into selective colleges and received academic scholarships.

She is especially proud, however, of her progress in science, technology, engineering and mathematics (STEM) classes, even though they were difficult for her. She is also "proud of having learned to work with my mind in ways that do not limit me."

Barry

Barry is a male student who received the labels of gifted, ASD, and ADHD, and was diagnosed with depression and an anxiety disorder. Barry has strong verbal abilities and thinking skills, especially in the area of synthesis. He is talented with translation, and can always position events within a historical or comparative context. The labeling of Barry as both gifted and disabled occurred over a period of time. Barry and his family both thought he was gifted at age 4 because of behavior at home. However, he was not formally identified by his school until age 8. His mother thought he had learning problems at age 5, but school personnel did not diagnose these problems right away, even though teachers noticed them by second grade. Barry was diagnosed as being on the autism spectrum at age 5, with ADHD and gifted added at age 6; anxiety disorder was added at age 8; and at age 12, depression was added to his profile.

From early on, Barry's learning strengths were pattern recognition, retention in preferred subjects, teaching others, and being organized. He was effective in the use of several strategies to combat his disabilities, including breaking down large tasks into component parts, creating organizational systems that worked for him, and taking frequent breaks.

In respect to services for his abilities, he qualified and participated in talent search programs at universities, center-based programs for gifted learners in schools, special classes at the secondary levels (honors and AP), and contests and competitions. He enjoyed special success with the National Statistics Competition.

Interventions included pull-out programs, work with school clinicians, parent instruction in selected areas, and mentorships and tutorials in areas of disability. Early on, Barry received occupational therapy, play therapy, psychiatrist consultation, neurodevelopmental pediatrician consultation, and therapeutic listening training. He also engaged in social skill development as a 2-year, out-of-school experience, with sessions including both Barry and his parents.

Interventions that were most effective were those that involved personal attention from a clinician in school. Barry said, "Working with school clinicians/a personal aide was a great help to me because it allowed me to take frequent breaks and learn organizational skills, as well as vent about problems in school." His mother added that the aide provided help with self-regulation, working with other children, and managing transitions. Social skills and occupational therapy were also helpful, according to Barry's mother. She also noted that gifted programming "provided needed intellectual challenge."

Teachers used several techniques that were helpful to Barry across the K–12 spectrum. His mother noted that the use of accelerated content was the most effective technique used at all levels of schooling, a perception that Barry shared as well. Additional classroom-level interventions of importance included extended or frequent breaks and preferred seating in the classroom. Also critical was the presence of a one-on-one aide at the elementary level. Flexible time, frequent breaks, and acceleration of content were all important at the middle school level. During high school, acceleration was the most useful technique, followed by flexible time and independent learning opportunities.

Teachers, however, were less effective in working with Barry in the following areas, as he explained:

> Writing/reflection and career exploration I personally found to be very ineffective. Career exploration often felt impersonal and disconnected, with the person leading it having minimal knowledge at best. Writing and reflection just [were] not very effective for me because writing is rarely enjoyable for me.

Barry's mother also noted that techniques such as shaming, positive reinforcement charts (which Barry viewed as "dumb"), and reward systems (none of which motivated him), were ineffective. She further commented that acceleration was a better motivator than any behavioral intervention.

Barry attained several accomplishments. Personal independent projects were a joy for him, matched by team competition awards. He also received testing awards in content areas, honor roll, acceptance into a selective college, school awards, and advanced course credits in honors and AP. Acceptance into a selective college and a score of 5 on the AP Biology exam made him the most proud.

Barry's view of the long-term effects of interventions for his abilities and disabilities was very positive. He said: "Extended time has helped provide me a more level playing field with other students and has helped me realize my true potential." He also spoke of the positive influence of out-of-school opportunities that he had: "Out-of-school interventions helped me learn adequate social skills despite having ASD and have greatly helped me in all facets of life as a result." Finally, he noted the powerful effect of the support of his aide at the elementary level: "Having a personal aide in elementary school not only helped me with my social skills but also is the reason I have above-average organizational skills currently."

Barry was accepted to a selective state university and plans to pursue studies with an interdisciplinary focus.

Ralph

Ralph is a male twice-exceptional student with coexisting disorders. He received many official labels on the special education side, yet he was never formally identified as gifted. He was diagnosed with ADHD, depression, ASD, oppositional defiant disorder, and bipolar disorder. All of these diagnoses were made outside of school by private psychologists.

His strength in school was in the area of history, about which he was passionate. He also enjoyed making interdisciplinary connections. He asked well-framed, thought-provoking questions in class and took advantage of all academic and extracurricular opportunities afforded to him through high school.

Ralph's family first saw him as gifted at age 6, based on his behavior at home. He taught himself to read, using Reader Rabbit, at age 5. By the end of first grade, he had read the entire first Harry Potter book. Learning problems also emerged at the same time. His father noted:

> He underwent a personality change around age 3. He began talking incessantly—he literally would talk virtually without stopping from the time he got up until the time he went to bed. When I was home, he would follow me around the house talking. He would frequently insist on my answering hypothetical, impossible questions, and then demand to know my reasoning when I answered. By age 5 or 6, he was having serious behavioral problems in school, which steadily worsened, everything from being disruptive in preschool and kindergarten to running away in the first grade.

To address his abilities in school, special opportunities for advanced coursework were provided for Ralph. In-school pull-out programs in academic areas and sessions with school clinicians were provided to address his disabilities. Yet neither had a strong impact on lessening his problems or enhancing his abilities.

Over the years, Ralph received multiple services in school for social and motor skills. However, they were not intensive enough. Ralph also had a negative attitude toward them and was not cooperative. His father commented further: "What was effective was the attention of highly dedicated teachers and administrators who devoted enormous amounts of time to him and his needs."

Personal interaction with teachers was the most effective intervention across all levels of development. Ralph and his family rated acceleration of content as second most effective. A third effective technique was the use of independent learning.

Both parents felt that their tracking of Ralph's homework assignments was critical to his surviving high school, even though it took a great deal of time and energy. They also felt that the high school offered little support for his needs. His parents stopped attending IEP meetings due to their uselessness and even perceived harm.

In regard to Ralph's progress in schooling, his father elaborated extensively on the role of interventions tried with his son:

> [I]t is not really clear to me that anything we did with Ralph was particularly effective. Over the years, in addition to the services we received through the school, we spent thousands of hours and tens of thousands of dollars on psychiatrists, psychologists, speech therapists, handwriting therapists, social skills classes, etc. Although I suppose that it is possible that these efforts had a cumulative, incremental effect that was too subtle and gradual for me to perceive, I would be hard-pressed to think of a single time that we saw visible improvement as a result of our actions. The one exception to this statement would be that, at least for several years, medication was quite literally the only thing that kept us going. I can no longer remember the exact timeframe, but from roughly the second grade through approximately the sixth, Ralph had frequent, uncontrollable explosions of anger—he repeatedly assaulted teachers and administrators throughout this period. We tried various combinations of medications and eventually settled on one that worked. . . . But at some point the medications apparently quit having an effect: Around the 10th grade, Ralph insisted upon quitting all medications, and I anticipated a catastrophe. Instead, nothing happened; there was literally no perceptible change. But during his most critical, desperate years, roughly first grade through seventh, there is no doubt in my mind he would have been expelled from school were it not for the medications.

His father further commented on Ralph's developmental process in the final years of high school:

> It is my belief that in the end such progress as he has made is primarily a function of maturity rather than our efforts. Beginning in approximately the 11th grade, his focus and organizational skills began slowly to improve; he is still disorganized, but it is not the pathological, mind-bending lack of organization that previously characterized him. During this time he also made the first friend he's had in many years—a deeply

troubled young woman who has had a negative effect on
him, but a friend, nonetheless.

One teacher ignored Ralph's IEP accommodations and bluntly refused to
work with him when he struggled in her class. However, he found a teacher of
the same subject on his own who was willing to work with him after school
and help him succeed on the final exam. He was more than willing to put in
the effort and the time to prepare himself for the challenges of the next year's
curriculum.

Despite fairly serious problems, Ralph received several awards for his performance in school. He received individual contest awards, team competition
awards, testing awards, honor roll, acceptance into a selective college, and advanced course credit from honors coursework. He earned gold medals on the
National Classical Etymology Exam and the National Roman Civilization
Exam for 3 years in a row, as well as honor certificates on the National Latin
Exam, attesting to his achievement at the national level.

Ralph was accepted to a small, selective university and reported his de-
light with the campus and intellectual environment. He plans to major in
history.

Rachel

Rachel is an identified gifted student who has suffered from diagnosed anxiety since age 8. She has a strong drive to succeed, a passion for knowledge, and intellectual curiosity. She believes that her "drive allows [her] to combat laziness."

She participated in many types of gifted programs, both pull-out and center-based. She also participated in Saturday and summer programs at universities in her area. She particularly enjoyed a mentorship in writing during her middle school years. Her best experience was placement in a gifted center where she could "function at a higher level when surrounded by others at equal or higher levels."

In her Latin classes, Rachel advocated for diverse viewpoints, such as those of slaves or women, which are often absent from the Latin curriculum. She did a brilliant job of putting together imagined responses to works of literature from different perspectives, such as Lesbia's responses to Catullus's poems, and never shied away from comparing the ancient to the modern. She studied different works of literature in greater depth (e.g., Cicero's *Pro Caelio*) by crafting her own poetry or speeches to respond to the usually patriarchal ones in the program of studies.

She also possessed dramatic flair, convincing her whole class to participate in a production of a Latin play for performance at an awards ceremony. For the performance, she not only directed but also cowrote an adaptation of a Plautus play, *The Menaechmi*, which was the basis for Shakespeare's *A Comedy of Errors*. Although Rachel experienced setbacks with the production due to her anxiety and perfectionism, she managed to succeed by researching other productions of both Plautus and Shakespeare. Through that process, she gained confidence in her understanding of the project and what was needed. The presentation, performed for 200 Latin students and parents, was a great success.

In respect to interventions that worked, Rachel felt that many were effective with her, noting that acceleration was a consistent help throughout her early years in school, along with one-on-one teacher time. She noted: "One-on-one teacher time led to very influential discussions with people whose opinion I valued." At the elementary level, she found that an emphasis on the arts, flexible use of time, social cueing, graphic organizers, and project-based learning with peers were all successful. At the secondary level, she mentioned opportunities for group discussion, independent study, career exploration, and question-asking as other effective approaches to her learning.

She commented on one of the most impactful approaches: "Question-asking increased my critical thinking skills."

Rachel did not enjoy large-group projects, as she felt "dragged down by others." Moreover, her mother suggested that Rachel did not thrive in narrowly defined learning situations:

> Assignments or environments in which there was only one path to success were not her thing. Achievement of learning goals and grades were important to her. If she is blocked, she will work to find another way. If there is no other path available, she is frustrated, and it is a waste of potential success (for her).

Rachel was rewarded for her drive to success with awards for her personal independent projects, team competition awards, honor roll, acceptance into selective programs, and advanced course credits in honors and AP. She was proudest of her award in eighth grade for being the best overall student.

She viewed her experiences in the gifted program as valuable and beneficial overall, even though she encountered some frustration as a result of increased perfectionistic tendencies. She found the program to be most effective in giving her the critical thinking skills necessary to be a confident independent thinker. She also found her special education accommodations helpful, as they were "socially impactful, led to increased empathy, and knowledge of social cues."

Rachel was accepted to a selective university and currently remains unsure about her major. She does plan to continue study of the theater and language, two areas of interest she explored during her high school years.

Charles

Charles is a male student, identified as gifted with the learning disability dysgraphia. He was formally identified as gifted at age 7 in second grade, when his dysgraphia was also diagnosed. Both his teachers and his mother recognized his abilities and disability at this early stage in development.

Charles identified the ability to absorb information quickly as one of his major strengths, along with "making intuitive leaps in thinking." He found that focusing over a period of time is a major problem for him, noting, "I need to space out my work in a rotation in order to keep myself engaged."

To address his giftedness, Charles participated in center-based programs for the gifted and contests and competitions, especially Math Olympiad, WordMasters, and Toastmasters. Accommodations for his disability included a pull-out program and a typing accommodation.

In his Latin classes, Charles was known for his sense of humor and enjoyment of satire, particularly in upper-level Latin classes, where he had a chance to parody the style of different writers. He regularly made connections to the sciences in class, when Latin or Greek informed nomenclature or scientific understanding.

Charles often challenged the thinking of other students and authorities (including the teacher and the textbook) but always in polite and appropriate ways. When other students were more focused on the specific translations of passages reviewed in class, Charles was anxious to relate the translations to the broader context of Vergil's message in *The Aeneid*, for example, making connections among the literature, language, history, and mythology. He was a prominent member of his school's academic team and helped that team reach the national championships for 2 years in a row. Charles took great pleasure in helping others to learn. For example, he was proudest of the fact that he founded the Science Olympiad at his school, "setting the groundwork in clubs and activities for new people to walk down."

He felt that he benefited greatly from summer enrichment programs as well as his center placement during the school year, noting that both "instilled love of learning, and the value of being un-ironically enthusiastic. They set me on a path to majors I planned to undertake in college." He also credited his gifted program with providing him "a hunger for knowledge and impatience at learning slowly."

Charles enjoyed three major approaches used by teachers to enhance his abilities. Regardless of grade level, these three were articulated as the most important: (1) questioning, (2) acceleration, and (3) independent study. Of the most effective approach, he said: "Question asking—a natural growth education led to learning as exploration rather than a chore." Yet he also found the power of individual teachers to be profound: "Every teacher I had a personal relationship with profoundly affected my growth." He also noted the long-term positive effects of out-of-school interventions on his continued growth.

Least enjoyable for Charles were assignments that were too structured and rigid: "Incredibly structured, strict requirements in formatting would frustrate me and make me wish to find loopholish alternate manners technically acceptable out of sheer contrarian moods and would also discourage my interest." His mother also noted the kind of work Charles did not enjoy: "Assignments with rigid structures and requiring medium-high levels of organization. The same was true of teaching styles—I believe he had much to contribute but required more of an open field to do so."

Charles noted that he had many accomplishments in school, including awards for his academics and testing prowess and his placement in contests and competitions. He had little opportunity for individualized support through a tutor or mentor, however.

He graduated from high school with a keen interest and ability to help other students who shared his giftedness and dysgraphia. He noted: "I work with the program now on the other side. I find myself repeating those things that my teachers told me because they helped me so much. . . . I have seen a difference in kids."

Charles went to a selective state university and graduated with a degree in physics. He is currently pursuing a career in teaching.

Commonalities Across the Profiles

Although all of these students differ in respect to their needs and talents, there are commonalities among them, and perhaps among many other students with special needs as well. It is important to note that all of these students in the reported case studies came to the attention of researchers because of their successful participation in an advanced Latin language program at the high school level. Although some of them were also advanced in other subject areas, clearly the 10 discussed are all advanced in their language skills. Other important commonalities are noted below, which provide a blueprint for thinking about interventions with learners with special needs.

1. **Identification.** According to research, students with special needs are underidentified for gifted services, at a ratio as high as 1 in 2 (NAGC, 2015). Yet for the majority of these students, identification came about through a challenging curriculum. A curriculum that forces students to think in complex ways and at an accelerated pace brings forth behaviors overlooked in other learning contexts. Moreover, the daily interactions that occur between teacher and learner across a multiyear period clearly accentuate the role of inquiry as a primary process to spur motivation and performance.

2. **Interventions.** All of the 10 students needed both academic and social-emotional interventions. On the academic side, each of them required different forms of acceleration, either within individual assignments or for a whole grade level. They also needed to work on metacognitive skill sets, such as planning and organizing, as well as

reflecting on their own learning. At the social-emotional level, these students needed to learn to take academic risks and to have an advocate who would be available to discuss coping mechanisms and special problems that arose in the academic sphere of their lives. At the conative level, these students needed to use their motivation in productive ways.

3. **Career guidance.** Students also needed career guidance provided by a knowledgeable counselor or career services specialist, as well as career-oriented advice and help with relevant skills from all teachers. Long-term planning, for example, was a critical skill needed among these students—to be able to see a few years ahead rather than just a few months. Approaches such as sharing information about education and career paths; discussing interview skills, job skills, and self-advocacy; and locating peers and mentors for students at varying stages of school can assist these students with this ongoing process.

4. **Teachers.** Teacher characteristics that these students responded to varied, but some were common among all. Students appreciated teachers who were open to trying new things, especially if they were student-selected or suggested. One student said, "Even if a strategy doesn't work, at least it lets you know they care enough to see if it does." Another said that he preferred teachers who were willing to teach to his strengths because "very few teachers see me for who I am if they teach me in [my area of weakness]." Another desirable teacher trait was patience: helping students work through their difficulties or disabilities, supporting them when they failed at something, and refusing to let them quit. The students all commented on the need for teachers who would help them succeed, allowing them freedom of choice wherever possible and focusing on what works for them as learners.

5. **Strengths.** Even though the nature of disabilities varied, all of these students had some form of disability or disabling condition, such as anxiety. Thus their giftedness was often overlooked, ignored, or seen as secondary when it came to educational interventions. All of these students found greater satisfaction and success from interventions that recognized and addressed their abilities than they did from remedial interventions. These students improved when teachers addressed their strengths without addressing areas of weakness directly.

6. **Language skills.** The nature of giftedness in each of the unidentified students ($N = 4$) was in the area of highly developed language skills, as their identification occurred in the Latin classroom at the high school level. The students' performance in Latin would clearly sug-

gest high-level abilities in language. Three of them were also labeled ASD, two were from poverty, and one had a severe physical disability; perhaps these factors precluded earlier identification.

7. **Financial difficulties.** Of the students from poverty who were in the study, all three faced special challenges after graduation from high school in respect to acquiring sufficient funds from scholarships to pay for college. All three considered a community college to be their only option at the outset. One was able to secure a full scholarship to a selective university as a transfer student. Another had advocates who helped her get full tuition to a selective 4-year institution. The third stayed at the community college and graduated with an associate's degree, unable to go on due to lack of funding. Thus, the commonality for all students from poverty appears to be the need for scholarship and transition support for college.

8. **Independent learning.** Positive outcomes were achievable when students engaged directly with their own learning, taking charge of its pace, style, and organization. Autonomy in learning then became the goal alongside the specific content and skill-based learning to be mastered.

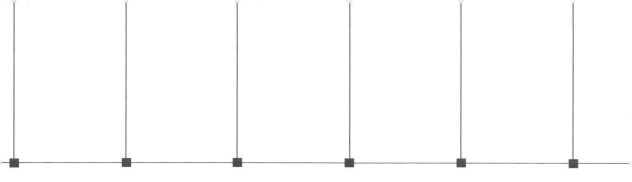

Talent Trajectories of Special Populations

Based on the data collection of 10 students who have finished high school, the following approaches were most successful in their talent trajectories:

1. **Early intervention.** Both parents and students were aware of giftedness before they were aware of a disability or special condition, usually no later than at age 8. This early knowledge provided the basis for parents to intervene positively in the lives of their children to promote their areas of strength. Thus, many of these students remember working with parents on skills and concepts and attending Saturday and summer enrichment programs at local universities as particularly enjoyable educational experiences during their primary years in school.

2. **Acceleration.** Most of the cases found acceleration to be the most effective intervention that was provided, as early as elementary school, and found that it continued to be effective all of the way through middle and high school. The acceleration model was typically in a subject area of strength, not whole-grade acceleration. The best outcomes occurred as a result of ongoing content-based acceleration and started well before secondary school. Honors and AP coursework options helped these students continue to experience acceleration at the secondary level. Another advantage of acceleration for these students was that it could be used continuously throughout the schooling process, with little additional effort on the part of the school establishment.

3. **Personalization.** For most of these students, some degree of personalization was required in order for them to perform at maximal levels throughout their years of schooling. For many of these students, this personalization involved finding the right teacher who could both motivate and support them in their area of interest to reach levels at which they did not think they could perform. In other instances, personalization involved a parent who provided needed support at propitious times. Often clinical support personnel were also crucial at various stages of development.

4. **Independent learning.** Independent learning was a preferred strategy over all forms of group learning. In fact, a few students rated independent learning as the most effective approach, and group learning as the least effective. Difficulties with finding intellectual peers made group work a source of constant frustration. On the other hand, students who were allowed to work on independent learning projects had more freedom of choice as well as personalized attention and feedback from the instructor that motivated them to do well with a topic of interest.

5. **Flexible instruction.** A common need among these students was flexibility of instruction. They encountered difficulties when faced with rigid classroom structures or assignments, and a few students reported defiant behavior as their immediate response. However, when given multiple pathways to success or alternatives to support their unique circumstances, these same students could perform at much higher levels of achievement.

Interventions were needed at key stages of the schooling process, as articulated by the students from the case studies. Table 1 illustrates the nature and variety of the interventions cited at each of these stages of development.

Table 1
Levels of Schooling Linked to Student-Identified Interventions

Level of Schooling	Opportunities for Intervention
Primary	One-on-one interactions Content acceleration
Intermediate	One-on-one interactions Content acceleration Ability grouping
Middle School	Project- and problem-based learning Content acceleration Ability grouping Contests and competitions Mentorships/tutoring
High School	Acceleration through Honors/Advanced Placement, etc. Opportunities for state/national contests Project- and problem-based learning College planning and career development Mentorships and/or internships in area of passion
Post-secondary	Advanced coursework in field of interest Attendance at selective university Mentorships/relationships with key experts

Issues and Problems for Special Populations in Schools and Gifted Programs

Giftedness is the characteristic that looms the largest in the profiles of these students, and it is the one that must be accommodated, regardless of the secondary or tertiary characteristics of each student. Unless giftedness is viewed as their primary characteristic, these students will not reach their ultimate potential. In the case studies examined, the interventions that have mattered have been ones focused on talent development (e.g., acceleration, independent learning, personal connection, flexibility, etc.). Many schools focus instead on the perceived weaknesses of these students—on language development as the primary goal for ELLs, on a learning disability such as dysgraphia, on background knowledge problems related to poverty, or on the minority status of a student. Yet it is the gifted profiles of these students that provide the most important data points on decision making for interventions at every stage of development.

For these students, the challenge of catching up from behind can seem insurmountable. These populations (ELLs, students of poverty, twice-exceptional students) must all conquer other circumstances (e.g., birth, language, disability) to function at a high level. Sometimes their profiles will appear flat, as the gifts are masked by circumstantial problems. The mechanism for helping these students is usually remediation, but acceleration should be tried, as it is more in line with their learning capacities and more likely to place them with students who are like them intellectually. Resistance to group settings is usually exacerbated by remedial treatment. Thus the use of acceleration in various forms and areas of the curriculum where these students excel is a critical intervention that can promote success in learning.

There is an even greater need for social-emotional support for these populations as they progress in their education. Gifted students in general have a well-documented need, but twice-exceptional students frequently face greater challenges in accessing the curriculum at the same level as their intellectual peers. The frustration of catching up from behind or continually having to prove themselves worthy of acceleration or inclusion in a class can generate great stress, as well as cultural or value conflicts at home. Thus, services that address affective needs, delivered by teachers and counselors working collaboratively, are an important part of the intervention options these students need at all levels of schooling.

One-on-one teacher mentorships and counseling can be protective factors that give students the opportunity to express their anxieties and solve emotional problems. These students also benefit disproportionately from having the same supportive adults, such as teachers and counselors, in their life across a period of multiple years. In the space of one academic year, teachers are hard-pressed to get to know the profiles of each individual student on their roster in time for effective planning, especially when a student's needs are both deep and diverse. Yet the teachers who encounter students across multiple years, as is common in language classrooms or elementary contexts where looping is used, can become more knowledgeable about student needs and better able to recommend interventions of value. Thus, the personal connections with teachers and other educators over years in school provide the best support for these students to grow at rates commensurate with their abilities.

Conclusion

Part I of this text has introduced the target populations of interest who constitute gifted learners with special needs, what is known about them, and the research base on their need for intervention. This first section of the book has also laid out important case studies for consideration of gifted learners with special needs, highlighting their strengths and areas for improvement, what interventions work for them in school and beyond, and the people in their lives that have mattered in their development.

The portrait that evolves from these studies shows the diversity of these students in respect to abilities, disabilities, and the issues they face in the talent development process. The needs of these populations may seem overwhelmingly complex, yet with careful targeted planning and the specific interventions suggested in Part II, their needs can be met.

PART II

What Interventions Work With Special Populations?

Adults can change their circumstances; children cannot. Children are powerless, and in difficult situations they are the victims of every sorrow and mischance and rage around them, for children feel all of these things but without any of the ability that adults have to change them. Whatever can take a child beyond such circumstances, therefore, is an alleviation and a blessing.

—Mary Oliver

Part II of this book explores the intervention practices that increase the likelihood that gifted learners with special needs will have opportunities that are an optimal match to their specialized abilities. The interventions that follow include: (1) approaches that may be used without consideration of the type of special needs the learner has and (2) approaches that may be most effective with one type of learner. One important consideration is that the needs of these learners change as they develop. For example, acceleration may be critical at some stages but not at others. Independent work may be a perfect approach at one level of learning but not at another. Careful ongoing assessment of needs must accompany the continued or new use of an intervention. Discussion of these differences in practice is provided as needed in the following commentary.

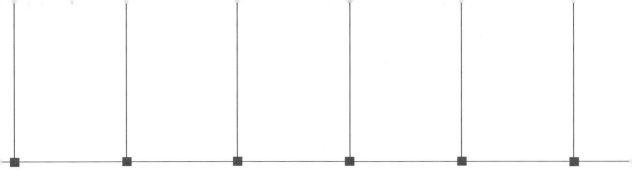

School-Based Interventions

Students in this research study identified four cross-categorical practices that helped them in their scholastic development: acceleration, personal relationships with teachers and other personnel, mentorships and internships, and career exploration (see Figure 1).

Of these four, acceleration in their strength areas was the most highly rated intervention by the students. The students noted that they received more accelerative opportunities in the secondary years but little in earlier stages of schooling. Actual research on effective interventions also supports the students' perceptions. Indeed, the research base on acceleration is overwhelmingly positive in all forms and at all levels of the schooling enterprise. Although acceleration is not routinely considered as an intervention for these kinds of students, it has proven to be the most effective.

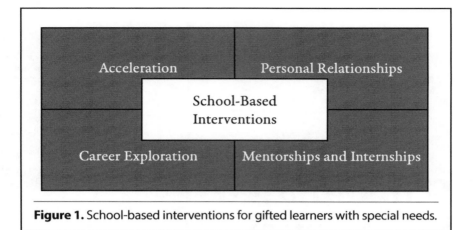

Figure 1. School-based interventions for gifted learners with special needs.

Acceleration in a Strength Area

Perhaps more has been written about the efficacy of accelerative practices with the gifted than about any other single educational intervention with any population. Reviews of the literature on acceleration have appeared with some regularity over the last 55 years (Assouline, Colangelo, VanTassel-Baska, & Lupkowski-Shoplik, 2015; Benbow, 1991; Colangelo, Assouline, & Gross, 2004a, 2004b; Daurio, 1979; Kulik & Kulik, 1984; Reynolds, Birch, & Tuseth, 1962). Each review has carefully noted the overall positive impact of acceleration on gifted individuals at various stages in the life span. Successful programs of acceleration, most notably the offshoots of the basic talent search model developed by Julian Stanley and others in the 1970s, have demonstrated and continue to demonstrate the significant positive impact of accelerative practices on student learning (Gross, 2004; Park, Lubinski, & Benbow, 2013; Steenbergen-Hu, Makel, & Olszewski-Kubilius, 2016; Swiatek & Benbow, 1991).

Some studies have focused on the positive effects of specific forms of acceleration. Brody (2004) found that among accelerated students, the best predictor of college achievement was early and continued Advanced Placement course-taking, suggesting that the challenging work of AP, applied on an ongoing basis, has a close correlation to later achievement. McClarty (2015) found overall positive effects for grade acceleration on college performance. Olszewski-Kubilius, Steenbergen-Hu, Thomsen, and Rosen (2017) demonstrated the long-term benefits of accelerated work for minority students, and Howley et al. (2015) conducted research showing the same benefits for rural students. These strong and consistent results suggest that the learners with special needs featured in this book have profited from acceleration and would have profited more from its routine use in areas where learning assessments supported it.

Across all three special needs populations studied in this book (twice-exceptional students, students of poverty, and ELLs), acceleration should be the first intervention applied—although acceleration profiles and patterns will look different in different students. It appears that at least one area of content acceleration should be considered each year as an appropriate intervention for these populations.

Elementary-Level Acceleration

At the elementary level, the following types of acceleration should be routinely considered:

- **Content-area acceleration.** Acceleration in an area of strength is a strategy for addressing the needs of most of these students. For example, students strong in verbal ability should be reading advanced texts with advanced vocabulary and discussing those texts with other students with comparable verbal aptitude. In math, students should be assessed for their level of math knowledge and skills, and should be advanced to appropriate levels with enriched problem-solving activities to augment their program of study. In science, these students should be given opportunities for designing and conducting experiments through a problem-based learning approach while being exposed to advanced readings and discoveries daily. What will vary is the degree and nature of the acceleration provided, based on individual student needs. Where possible, these students should be integrated with other gifted learners in a special grouped setting, which might be a special class, a cluster, or a dyad.
- **Mentoring and tutoring.** These accelerative activities may also prove to be useful for these students. Because individual assistance requires the tutor to assess the level of functioning in a designated area of need, most of these one-on-one relationships involve a degree of acceleration in the strength area.
- **Contests and competitions.** Competitions can also prove helpful in advancing these students in the application of their skill sets. Engagement in these types of activities elevates the learning to an advanced level and demonstrates for these students how accomplished they are in a given skill set.

Secondary-Level Acceleration

At the secondary level, the following acceleration provisions should be considered annually:

- **Early entrance to high school subjects.** Early entrance may be an important consideration for these students, especially in areas such as second languages and math. Second language learning should not be restricted to those who are linguistically talented, nor should it be denied to ELLs, who can often find a formula for English language learning in the foreign language classroom (VanTassel-Baska, MacFarlane, & Baska, 2017). Math has traditionally been the subject of choice for acceleration, although not typically for these types of learners. It is an excellent choice if the student is mathematically able enough to handle the preassessment for entry into the program.

- **Continued work in contests and competitions.** Many of these competitions only begin at the secondary level (e.g., Science Olympiad, Poetry Out Loud, National History Day). As students with special needs become more familiar with competition formats, some of them may really excel. For example, students with visual impairments may perform well in a contest where speed of processing matters in hitting a buzzer, as these students are not deterred by visual distractions.
- **Advanced work in all core subjects for which students show readiness.** Moving students into honors and Advanced Placement earlier than typical is an example of orchestrating this advancement in subjects. For example, students with strengths in verbal areas may opt for AP Language and Composition during their freshman and sophomore years if they have demonstrated readiness in their reading and writing abilities.
- **Independent work.** Students can work independently on advanced content in a core area for which they demonstrate both interest and ability. For example, a student may take the next year of a course independently where appropriate, using a learning assessment that documents proficiency.

Personal Relationships With Teachers and Other Personnel

Building personal relationships with students is almost universally acknowledged as a best practice in teaching (Fecho, 2004). Teacher efficacy as measured in the teacher evaluation process is often linked to the ability to connect with student interests and respond to individual needs (Baum, Owens, & Dixon, 2017). The gifted education standards also call for addressing the affective needs of these students through forging personal relationships (Johnsen, 2012). Siegle (2013) suggested that the development of a personal rapport with students is a crucial pathway in motivating underachieving gifted individuals, a group that includes many students with special needs. What are the general approaches, then, that educators may develop and implement at the personal level?

Establish rapport. Teachers can give their students interest surveys at the beginning of the year and follow up with them through conversations about how to address those interests, either in upcoming schoolwork (projects or other activities that allow choice) or extracurricular events planned in the school or regional area.

Communicate regularly in regard to progress. Although students must be monitored for progress, many times gifted learners with special needs are not supervised to ensure that they are on a growth path. Reasons vary but often center around these students' capacity to "get by" in the system. Ensuring that these students are experiencing growth is a critical part of a teacher's job with the gifted. Growth is assessed not only for performance on state tests, but also for national level comparisons with top learners in a given area.

Encourage students to persist with learning goals. Teachers may assist with developing the skills of persistence and resilience in these learners, first by helping them to see the progress they have already made, and then making sure to celebrate those successes. As students consider future goals, they may need to evaluate their own learning through processes such as metacognition to reflect on what contributed to past learning successes and what can get them through current stumbling blocks (Dixon & Moon, 2015).

Provide recommendations for special opportunities. Teachers may find ways to provide extracurricular assistance that is responsive to the interests and/or needs of these students. For example, one middle school teacher paid the commuter fare for one of her students from the inner city to participate in a free instrumental music program on Saturdays for which he had no transportation. Another teacher gave rides to a student who did not have transportation to state-level competitions. Still another teacher found an academic opportunity for her student, identified an appropriate scholarship to enable participation, and wrote the recommendation letters needed for the scholarship.

Respond to social-emotional needs. Some students' affective needs may be exacerbated by their exceptionalities. Teachers may have conversations with these students as needs arise. When students trust someone, they find solace in discussing the nature of their problems and how they might address them (Dixon & Moon, 2015). For example, Carla (see p. 29) spoke with a trusted teacher on a daily basis before school hours to address anxieties regarding school performance and to receive friendly encouragement. Ralph (see p. 34) also spoke with a teacher, but only on topics of interest, not personal affective concerns. Ralph's father indicated that this personal interaction was a necessary component for Ralph's development, although it was not an explicit intervention. Building relationships with these students may be as important as problem solving with them.

Mentorships and Internships

Mentorships

Mentorships offer structured program opportunities for gifted students to appreciate the nature of collaborative work in the sciences and other fields of endeavor. Researchers have found, for example, that many highly creative persons who have made a significant contribution in their field had a mentor to guide them in the processes, culture, and accepted practices of the field. Mentors are needed at different times and usually at different transition periods (Subotnik & Steiner, 1994). A good mentor is one who can nurture curiosity, self-efficacy, interests, and motivation in students (Miller, 2002). Patterns of successful mentorships also include a strong student interest in the project to be studied, voluntary selection of the mentor/mentee, and, most importantly, constructive feedback from the mentors (VanTassel-Baska & Subotnik, 2004). For gifted learners with special needs, the most helpful mentor may be one who has a pragmatic view of the world and how the student may best fit into the professional world of his or her interest.

Successful mentor programs in the sciences are a staple at specialized secondary schools for the gifted, such as Thomas Jefferson High School for Science and Technology in Virginia, the Illinois Mathematics and Science Academy, or similar programs in Singapore. In each of these programs, mentors are trained to work with students on selected scientific and technological projects of interest to the students. The mentors typically have a background in the area of the project and work at a lab or university that is conducting similar research. The students have been preselected for their capacity to work collaboratively on projects and bring them to completion, as well as for their skill level in science and math. Typically, these mentorships last a semester or a whole year, depending on the project and the personnel involved. Project work is then displayed for a public audience and judged for its utility in answering real-world questions of interest on the topic under study.

In more recent years, the addition of STEM programs at the middle school level has hastened the development of project-based skills for gifted learners, as well as the 21st-century skill set that includes innovative thinking. In these programs, engineers and scientists serve as mentors who guide the development of projects.

Table 2
Benefits of Intern Placements

Intern Placements	Benefits to Students
Hospitals	• Exposure to routines and procedures • Project work • Access to a variety of career professionals (e.g., doctors, nurses, technicians) whose work may be of interest
Laboratories	• Exposure to conducting experiments • Collaborative teamwork • Access to professionals in interdisciplinary fields
Veterinary clinics	• Experience with handling animals • Exposure to protocols for animal research • Observation of the activities of veterinarians
Government agencies	• Experience with contracting work (e.g., language, bidding, etc.) • Proposal writing • Meeting with client/stakeholder groups

Internships

Offering opportunities for practical work experience in a field of interest may be one of the most important ways to help many gifted learners with special needs. The ability to tie real-world experiences back to school-based learning can keep interest alive and help students see connections between school and work. Learning about a career field by doing the work itself, even at a lower level, offers important insights into how a future career path might be crafted. Connecting to people who have expertise in related areas is also helpful. For example, students may gain experience working in labs by interning at a national or corporate lab site. Through such internships, they also might gain experience in using the related skills of mathematical reasoning and technological competencies. Table 2 lists the types of intern placements that may prove helpful to students, as well as the potential benefits of each placement.

The more personalized the internship setting, the more that students with special needs will feel comfortable in it. Helping them to develop relationships within their setting and to see the need for establishing a professional network is a role for teachers who are coordinating these activities. Contracts are useful to ensure that the benefits to students are explained and that experiences are varied and educational.

Career Exploration

This intervention was rated highly, particularly for the twice-exceptional students and students from poverty, in this book's study. The research literature also supports using career exploration regularly with students with ASD and students with specific learning disabilities to ensure that they have ideas for how to convert interests and abilities into real-world careers (Weinfeld et al., 2013). Career exploration is also critical for low-income students, who often associate career paths with those of their parents who may not have attended college (Wyner, Bridgeland, & DiIulio, 2007). Career planning targeted to the gifted learner may not be provided as a part of the overall services to the gifted population, let alone to learners with special needs (Swiatek & Benbow, 1991). Thus, models for developing skills in career planning may prove useful for educators to employ in their work with special populations (McDonald & Farrell, 2012; Wood & Lane, 2017).

The nature of career exploration may come in many forms and from several sources:

- Guest speakers could share information about their careers, how to enter specific fields, what activities make up the majority of their time, and what their perspectives were when they were secondary school students. Real-world contact with adults with whom students can identify may be invaluable in bolstering the confidence of these learners. Speakers who have experience being a minority, living in poverty, or living with a disability may be particularly helpful in inspiring students with special needs to believe that they, too, can secure high-level jobs in adulthood.

- Special seminars focusing on what careers are available and what professionals do on a daily basis could be organized. A panel of professionals (typically three adults) who all work in a related field, such as medicine, law, or education, can provide insight into the variety of roles available under the professional label. Students may learn, for example, that medical career paths have mushroomed since the advent of genetic research, opening up opportunities that did not exist a few years before.

- A sample lesson plan to aid in career exploration might be created. See Figure 2 for a general example.

- Reading biographies and autobiographies of professionals in fields of interest, like science, mathematics, writing, anthropology, or other areas of the arts, is a stimulating way to think about the life behind

Career Exploration Lesson Plan

Purpose: To explore career (or college) options.

Outcomes: Students will be able to compare and contrast different careers to make an informed decision.

For gifted students who have already chosen an intended career, this provides a dedicated time during which they can look at other options. For multipotential or undecided gifted students, it allows them to weigh pros and cons of possible choices. For special needs students who are gifted, it provides a way of connecting their current learning to possible futures in their designated areas of strength.

Focus topics: The following topics are recommended to focus the research activity: (a) describe what someone in that career does every day, (b) level of education/training required, (c) growing field or diminishing field, (d) average pay across country (and in state), (e) working indoors/outdoors/amount of travel required, and (f) independent or collaboration with others.

Time: The time frame for this lesson can vary from one class period to several periods, depending on the depth desired by students, teachers, and counselors.

Process description: Students choose three careers about which they are interested in learning more information. Students can then use the Internet to learn more about their chosen careers. Internet sites such as http://onetonline.org and the Occupational Outlook Handbook (http://www.bls.gov/ooh) are good resources to supplement career programs such as Naviance that may have been purchased by the school district. Students should organize their research in some way (e.g., notecards, Word documents, legal pads) and be able to share where they obtained the information.

Product: The final product is a written or oral presentation of findings and a final selection, along with a rationale, of a career for more in-depth study.

Figure 2. Model lesson plan for career exploration. From "Using the Integrated Curriculum Model to Address Social, Emotional, and Career Needs of Advanced Learners" by S. M. Wood and E. M. D. Lane, in *Content-Based Curriculum for High-Ability Learners* (3rd ed., p. 531), by J. VanTassel-Baska and C. A. Little (Eds.), 2017, Waco, TX: Prufrock Press. Copyright 2017 by Prufrock Press. Reprinted with permission.

a career path. Too often, students choose careers that they will not realistically pursue because they are too demanding (e.g., 80-hour weeks in a science lab to conduct original research) or because they are incompatible with a person's temperament (e.g., a solitary career like writing as opposed to one that requires working with people). *Composing a Life* by Mary Catherine Bateson (daughter of Margaret Mead and Gregory Bateson) is an excellent example of a book that helps gifted individuals see the big picture in this kind of planning.

- Career issues also are important to share with parents and may provide a basis for important conversations. The following questions offer a forum for online or in-person seminar discussions with parents on career development concerns:
  1. What do you see as the central problem(s) in helping your child begin to consider careers?
  2. How important is outstanding ability in an area as a basis for a successful career? Can it compensate for other nonintellective factors that an individual may not have?
  3. Studies of eminent individuals in several fields suggest that hard work, commitment to a field, and curiosity are the best predictors for doing creative work. How does your child view work ethic as a part of developing talent?
  4. What mechanisms have worked best thus far in guiding your child to develop his or her abilities? What interventions have provided important milestones on the road to choosing a career?
  5. Gifted students typically make very early career decisions (even in the primary years) or very late ones (post undergraduate). What concerns do you have about your child's timing in career decision making?

The overall strategies, then, for career development include an emphasis on the use of seminars, guest speakers, parental discussions of career opportunities, and outside real-world experiences.

Just as acceleration, personal connection, mentorship and internship programs, and career exploration were perceived by all participants in the study to be effective interventions, so too have selective classroom interventions. The next section on interventions explores classroom strategies that may be employed to enhance learning for these learners.

Classroom-Based Interventions

Gifted students with special needs across several areas of labeling identified the following approaches to learning as helpful for them at the primary, intermediate, and secondary levels. These five inquiry-based approaches (see Figure 3) are presented in the following format: (1) a description of the strategy, (2) a model lesson that may be used as a prototype by teachers, and (3) tips for teachers in implementing the strategy at the classroom level.

Problem-based learning especially was noted as effective if conducted independently or with students with similar abilities. The Literature Web was most useful as a visual aid to learning, providing a welcome alternative to auditory-only approaches in the classroom, such as lecture or discussion. Higher level questioning/thinking sensitized students to the types and levels of questions that would be asked of them but also helped them realize that they could ask about any area of study. The use of creative expression offered these students opportunities for choice and flexibility in the assignments. Finally, the use of the arts provided interdisciplinary connections across subjects in both core and noncore areas.

Inquiry-Based Learning

Why is inquiry an important umbrella for instructional interventions? Inquiry provides multiple benefits for gifted learners with special needs. First of all, it stimulates thinking that promotes more questioning and more prob-

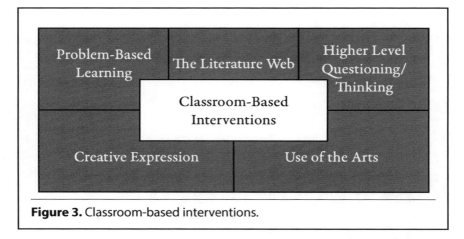

Figure 3. Classroom-based interventions.

ing to understand a topic or phenomenon. Inquiry processes also allow for students to clarify what others—both teachers and fellow students—have said in the classroom (Coleman & Johnsen, 2013). Often students with special needs may not process a conversation or discussion to the extent necessary to think deeply about issues. Asking students to generate clarification questions and giving time to ask them and respond can alleviate that problem. These students may also have the need to be open in their approach to learning, which implies that the search for understanding should be as unfettered as possible. Finally, imbuing a sense of wonder in these students about the tentativeness of knowledge is a central learning tenet.

Gifted learners with special needs require more open-ended opportunities for learning where the answers are not preordained. By the same token, they need more activities that allow for creative expression where they can enjoy real-world problem solving.

Scaffolds for Elevating Learning

Students also need tools, such as scaffolding, to understand their own learning patterns (Baska & VanTassel-Baska, 2016). Based on the case studies presented in this book, teachers may provide general scaffolds to promote higher level inquiry in these students. Scaffolds provide students with skills in problem finding and problem solving, as well as the underlying thinking skills that accompany such work, all in a supportive environment that boosts self-esteem.

The following types of activities engage and motivate learners to become self-directed in their inquiry and solution-finding strategies in life as well as in school. With the teacher acting as a facilitator and coach rather than a lecturer, students can explore options on their own and gain insight into their own learning habits, strengths, and areas for growth.

The teacher guides students to:

- ask questions about learning needs and accommodations that would work for them;
- research various topics to understand content and to make decisions;
- generate resolutions for their perceived problems that are feasible;
- refine personal problem-solving strategies to make skills more effective and efficient through self-evaluation;
- apply creative and critical thinking skills to problem-solving behaviors; and
- display positive attitudes to enhance self-regard.

Problem-Based Learning

One model that promotes inquiry and higher level problem solving is problem-based learning, a curriculum and instructional model that is highly constructivist in design and execution. First used in the medical profession to socialize doctors to real-world patient concerns, problem-based learning is now selectively employed in educational settings at elementary and secondary levels with gifted learners (Gallagher & Stepien, 1996).

The aspects of problem-based learning that distinguish it from other inquiry approaches may be summarized by the following points:

- Students are in charge of their own learning. Working in small investigatory teams, they grapple with a real-world, unstructured problem that they must solve within a short period of time. Students become motivated to learn because they are in charge at every stage of the process.

- The problem statement is ambiguous, incomplete, and yet appealing to students because of its real-world quality and the stakeholder role that students assume. For example, students may be given roles as scientists, engineers, politicians, or important project-based administrators whose job it is to deal with the problem expeditiously.

- The teacher plays a facilitative role rather than a directive one, aiding students primarily through asking questions and providing additional scaffolding of the problem with new information or resources needed. The teacher becomes a metacognitive coach, urging students through probing questions to deepen their inquiry.

- The students complete a Need to Know board early in their investigation that allows them to plan out how they will attack the problem, first by identifying what they already know from the problem statement, what they need to know, and how they will find out the information. They then can prioritize information, make assignments, and set up timelines for the next phase of work. Such an emphasis on constructed metacognitive behavior is central to the benefits of problem-based learning.

- Many times problems are constructed around specific situations involving pollution of water or air, dangerous chemicals, spread of infectious disease, or energy source problems. Students learn that the real world is interdisciplinary in orientation, requiring the use of many different thinking skills and many different kinds of expertise to solve problems.

- To work through a problem-based learning episode, students must be able to analyze, synthesize, evaluate, and create—all higher level thinking tasks.

The following lesson provides an example of a problem-based learning episode. It illustrates the principles of problem-based learning and demonstrates how this inquiry approach begins in the classroom.

Model Lesson 1: Problem-Based Learning

Instructional purpose:
- To collaborate on a real-world problem

Activity: Ask students to work in groups of 3–5 on the problem provided and create a complete Need to Know board (1 period). The following problem and its levels of complex thinking are illustrative of a problem-based learning episode.

> **Problem:** There is a lack of mass transit into and out of a central city. You are an urban planner, given one month to come up with a viable plan. However, your resources have been used on another project, that of city beautification. A new airport is about to be built 20 miles outside of the city, but negotiations are stalled. What do you do?

Higher level skills needed to address the problem include the following:
1. Analysis of what the real problem is—mass transit, airport construction, beautification?
2. Synthesis of the aspects of the problem—is there a creative synthesis of each facet of the problems noted?
3. Evaluation of alternative strategies to be employed—can I shift funds, can I employ a transportation expert, can I renegotiate the airport arrangements?
4. Creation of the plan of action that will need to be sold to city council.

Model Lesson 1: Problem-Based Learning, continued.

In groups, students proceed to address the problem by creating a Need To Know board that allows them to articulate what they know about the problem, what they need to know in the form of questions or inferences, and how they will find out the information. As they collaboratively develop their board, students will come to see the underlying patterns in the problem and how it needs to be organized for successful resolution.

Often interactions with a real-world expert or a visit to relevant labs or plants in the community can add reality and vividness to the problem details.

Assessment: A plan of action assessment by a real-world panel of experts (locally procured). For example, city managers could critique the plan according to criteria they would use if it were being considered for funding.

Note. Adapted from "Teaching Leadership Skills to Gifted Learners: Lessons in Tomorrow," by J. VanTassel-Baska, in *Content-Based Curriculum for High-Ability Learners* (3rd ed., p. 420), by J. VanTassel-Baska and C. A. Little (Eds.), 2017, Waco, TX: Prufrock Press. Copyright 2017 by Prufrock Press. Adapted with permission.

Research Skills

All problem-based and project-based learning requires that students do research, a skill set often overlooked in preparing gifted students to be independent in their learning habits. The teaching of research skills is all about question-asking, both the starting point of selecting a topic or issue and the ending point of asking "so what?" in determining implications of findings. The following model lesson introduces students to a question template that guides them through the inquiry process in their own group or independent research efforts.

Model Lesson 2: Research Skills

Instructional purposes:
- To introduce an inquiry-based research template
- To provide a scaffold for developing a research proposal

Activity: Ask students to respond to the following questions as they create a research proposal for consideration.

- **What do you want to know about an issue or topic?** Students need to generate a list of questions about their proposed research topic or issue.
- **What questions have priority?** Students need to rate the questions in order of greatest importance. Some questions may be clustered for rating purposes.
- **What prior studies will inform your work?** Students need to identify 12 references that relate to the topic or issue to be studied.
- **What methodology will help you best answer those questions?** Students need to identify the methodology they will employ in their study—the instrumentation to be used, as well as the data collection and analysis procedures to be employed.
- **How will you design your study?** Students need to determine participants in the study, the study's scope, and the limitations of the study.
- **What are your results and findings?** Students will need to state how they will report their findings for an audience. What data charts will be necessary? What tables will be needed?
- **What do the findings imply for practice and future research?** Students will need to draw implications for the application of the findings to classrooms and to future studies.

Note for teachers. It would be useful for students to have prior access to selected websites on topics of interest. The purpose of the lesson is to create an intellectual proposal, not to surf the web for resources. By preselecting useful websites for students, that concern is reduced.

Model Lesson 2: Research Skills, continued.

Assessment: Students may self-assess their research proposal, using the following criteria:

- Quality of response to the questions provided
- Organization of the proposal
- Originality of proposal ideas
- Coherence of the overall proposal

Tips for Teachers

The following practical suggestions for implementation provide teachers more ideas for using these archetypal lessons effectively. The tips have been field-tested in the classroom, and teachers have found them helpful when implementing these lessons with gifted learners with special needs. Although all groups may benefit from the problem or issue provided, gifted learners with special needs receive added benefits from both the problem stimulus and the activities and questions that are embedded in the templates they will use to respond, such as the Need to Know Board. Consider using contracts when working with students who are doing independent or small-group work for more than a week. An example of a contract to use or modify for this purpose may be found in Appendix B.

☑ Be strategic about grouping students for any form of project lasting more than a day. Use preassessment data as part of the decision but also ensure that gifted learners are grouped together regardless of disability or condition.

☑ Ensure that students understand the rubric on which their work will be assessed and that they use it as a guide to develop the project.

☑ Monitor student progress on projects by walking around the room and asking questions that students may have overlooked, rather than providing answers. Your role is that of metacognitive coach rather than traditional teacher.

☑ Need to Know boards work best if wall space is available for students to put up butcher block paper or white boards. In this way, students can see each other's work and monitor the changes made over time in the posted Need to Know boards as more data are collected.

☑ Teachers need to allocate both in-class and out-of-class time for successful implementation of problem-based learning and research projects. All supplies necessary for project completion need to be provided in the classroom, as students from poverty may not be able to access them outside. Research and writing can be done outside the classroom as homework, but group discussions and planning require classroom access for students.

The Literature Web

The Literature Web is a graphic organizer that deliberately engages students in a set of thinking processes that move from simple to complex, but it also involves different modes of thinking. The web moves from focusing on key words, to feelings about the text, to ideas conveyed in it, to symbols and images portrayed, to the structure used by the author to convey meaning. The thinking progresses from a tight focus on basic vocabulary to how the text affects the reader and impacts understanding at the abstract levels of theme, symbol, and linguistic composition.

This shared inquiry approach, developed as the Literature Web model, relies primarily on a core set of questions constructed by the teacher ahead of time to guide discussion of a specific reading or core stimulus related to a relevant topic (VanTassel-Baska & Little, 2017). Art objects and literature may be used to provoke discussion. Shared inquiry may or may not feature question probes (e.g., asking students "why" or " explain your reasoning") or follow-up assignments. Emphasis is placed on a careful search for meaning in the text-based reading or visual media, and student reactions to it. Based loosely on the shared inquiry process of *Junior Great Books,* the technique involves five steps, moving from simple to complex interpretation of the text or visual stimulus provided:

1. Students come up with words found in the text or images in the art piece that interest them, that they are curious about, and/or that they find important in understanding the stimulus.
2. Students declare their overall feelings about the stimulus, including how they react to it, whether they respond favorably or unfavorably, and why.
3. Students articulate the main ideas they think the author/artist is trying to convey with the text/art object.
4. Students discuss images and symbols that the artist is working with in the piece. What metaphors are used? What pictures come to mind?
5. Students comment on the structure of the artwork as it reinforces the intended meaning. What artistic and literary devices does the author employ?

In conducting the discussion, the facilitator should present the stimulus on an overhead projector or computer and provide students with a web that requires their response to each of the five areas delineated (see Figure 4). During stage one of the activity, students should traverse all five aspects of the web individually. During stage two of the process, students should work in

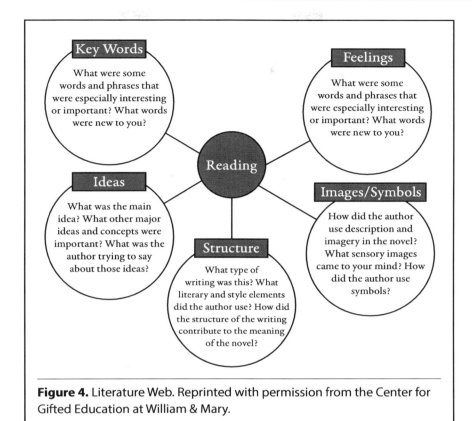

Figure 4. Literature Web. Reprinted with permission from the Center for Gifted Education at William & Mary.

Model Lesson 3: Using the Literature Web

Instructional purpose:
- To engage learners in using the arts to understand themselves, others, and life issues

Activities:
1. Ask students to view John Everett Millet's "Mariana" and then to read Alfred, Lord Tennyson's poem by the same name.
2. Have students explore each work separately, using the Literature Web as a guide. The web questions can be adapted for artistic works.

Model Lesson 3: Using the Literature Web, continued.

3. Discuss the insights gained through the web exploration in small groups and then as a whole group.
4. Ask students to write a comparison of the two works, based on their web responses.
5. Ask students to reflect on the following questions:
    ◆ How does the theme of "longing" pervade both works?
    ◆ What changes occur in understanding as one moves from one art form to another?

6. Have students use the following questions to think through ideas about the concept of change. Then, ask them to create a poem and visual that reflect a state of change they are experiencing in their lives.
    ◆ How does the concept of change apply to your life now?
    ◆ What evidence do you have that it is occurring?
    ◆ What is your perspective on whether the change is good or bad?

Assessment: Facilitators may wish to collect three webs from students throughout the course of their study, demonstrating their internalization of the process. Students should also be encouraged to include webs in their portfolios. After using this approach a few times, instructors may wish to ask students to comment on how the web encourages them to express feelings about what they encounter and how it helps them process those feelings within a cognitive framework.

Note. Adapted from "Secondary Affective Curriculum and Instruction for Gifted Learners" by J. VanTassel-Baska, J. S. McIntosh, and K. L. Kearney, in *The Handbook of Secondary Gifted Education* (2nd ed., pp. 524–525), by F. A. Dixon and S. M. Moon (Eds.), 2015, Waco, TX: Prufrock Press. Copyright 2015 by Prufrock Press. Adapted with permission.

dyads to discuss each web and compare their findings. During stage three, the facilitator should hold a whole-group discussion to determine the multiple insights gleaned through the process.

A lesson that uses two art forms and applies the scaffold of the Literature Web can elevate thinking about both poetry and the visual arts to higher and more abstract levels. The same web can also be used to elevate understanding of themes in works by different multicultural writers. The following model lesson provides options for students reading works by authors from different cultural backgrounds who tackled the same theme of "identity" in their work.

Model Lesson 4: Multicultural Author Study

Instructional purposes:
- To provide students access to multicultural authors
- To develop an understanding of the concept of identity

Activity: Read a short story, essay, or poetry by an African American, Hispanic American, and Asian American author.

Here is a list of possible authors to choose from. Please select one from each column and read at least one selection form each. In the case of a poet, read two poems by the same author.

African American	Hispanic American	Asian American
Gwendolyn Brooks	Sandra Cisneros	Carlos Bulosan
Langston Hughes	Isabel Allende	Peter Ho Davies
Lorraine Hansberry	Julia Alvarez	Anita Desai
Toni Morrison	Rudolfo Anaya	David Henry Hwang
Maya Angelou	Oscar Hijuelos	Maxine Hong Kings-
James Baldwin	Maria Hinojosa	ton
Phillis Wheatley	Geraldo Rivera	Chang-Rae Lee
	Luis Santeiro	Amy Tan
	Gary Soto	Lin Yutang

- Write in your journal what you learned about each culture from your readings.
- Read the biography or autobiography of one author whose work you have read. How does the author's life influence his or her writing?
- Create a concept map of the major theme of identity as it was explored in the work and life of your author (see the following example).

Model Lesson 4: Multicultural Author Study, continued.

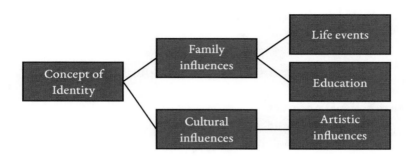

- Now create an artistic representation of the theme of identity that your authors may have experienced in their lives and expressed in their work. You may write a play, a short story, a poem set of three, a mural or collage, or a painting to express the idea. Your artistic piece should be accompanied by an artistic statement that indicates how the theme was used in the work you read.

Assessment: Use a product assessment that considers organization, content, creative ideation, and coherent representation on a 4-point scale, with 4 being high.

Tips for Teachers

The following practical suggestions for implementation provide teachers with more ideas to use these archetypal lessons effectively.

- ☑ Provide blank copies of the Literature Web for student use after you have introduced and used the scaffold with the whole group. Complete the web in class together and discuss it.
- ☑ The Literature Web has also been found to be useful as a tool for students to complete homework. Using the web to analyze a story may be a more useful homework assignment than a set of questions.
- ☑ For younger students, provide blank lines under questions so that they understand where they should place responses and that multiple responses are desirable.

☑ Have students do a peer review of each other's Literature Webs to gain insight into the similarities, differences, and interconnections of each other's ideas. This should be done before they begin writing.

☑ Have students articulate their webs in oral and/or written form. Either form should be acceptable, especially for ELLs and twice-exceptional students, who may prefer a presentation to a written report.

☑ Make sure the final product rubric is clear, regardless of the format selected. It should be focused on content and organization of ideas rather than other criteria, so that learners with special needs have opportunities to shine.

Higher Level Questioning/Thinking

In order to promote a broad-based approach to higher level thinking, teachers must introduce different types of questions for students to respond to, depending on the nature and level of thinking desired in each student (Beck & McKeown, 2007). Questions may be both teacher-generated and student-generated. Teachers should provide questions as a model for students to replicate as appropriate. Preparation of questions should focus on generating clusters of 4–6 questions for each text or visual stimulus (e.g., a poem or a painting) to be discussed. Any question may be the basis for a question probe, where a follow-up question is asked for clarification or to seek additional information. Sometimes "why" questions work well as a follow-up probe to a student response. Interpretive questions should always be considered for a question cluster, as they can reveal what is not understood in a situation, text, or scenario. Teachers must also consider the levels of the questions they are using, from lower to higher order, and how to achieve the best mix and balance (Hughes, Kettler, Shaunessy-Dedrick, & VanTassel-Baska, 2014).

The following model lesson allows students to explore different types and levels of questions and the purposes behind questions asked. It also allows them to create their own questions from lower to higher level and from memory to evaluation in type.

Model Lesson 5: Questioning

Instructional purpose:
- To introduce types of questioning

Activities: The following questions may be presented to students as a set for consideration as to their type, effectiveness, and balance.
- Why did you decide to stay out all night?
- Who were you with?
- What if you ran out of gas? What would have happened?
- What will be the effects of your behavior last night on your performance today?
- Which is worse—to miss out on some fun or not be able to do your best each day? Why?

Model Lesson 5: Questioning, continued.

Now discuss with students the basic types of questions that may be used to generate mostly higher level questions. The four-question strategy includes the following levels:

- Memory/Cognition—lower level questions that answer basic factual accounts, such as "who," "what," "when," and "where."
- Convergent—higher level questions that probe multiple causes and components, which often begin with "why" or "how."
- Divergent—higher level questions that are hypothetical and therefore open-ended in respect to intended response, beginning with the prompts "what if" or "pretend."
- Evaluative—higher level questions that are evaluative, asking students to decide "which is better or best" or develop criteria for judging a situation or event.

Students may now select one of the following topics and prepare a set of questions, using the four-question strategy:

- systems of government
- nuclear energy
- language study
- classroom rules and procedures

An example using the topic of *animal habitats* follows.

Memory/ Cognition Level	What is a habitat? What are different kinds of habitats?
Convergence Level	What factors influence choice of habitat? How does weather affect habitat?
Divergence Level	What if predators were eliminated? What impact would that have? What if the earth's axis tilted? What impact would that have?
Evaluative Level	How would you judge the infringement of humans on animal habitats?

Once students have an appreciation for the different types of questions that might be asked about any topic or issue, it is useful for them to participate in the highest level of seminar model that uses questioning as its core approach to learning.

Socratic Seminars

Socratic seminars are especially useful in the context of exploring real-world issues and concerns. The Socratic seminar is based on a model of inquiry where the group leader assumes the role of question-asker and question-prober but never provides an answer for any of the questions. Rather, he or she leads students to explore the issue among themselves to arrive at answers. Popularized by Mortimer Adler (1982) through his Paideia Proposal, the technique is used by teachers of the gifted predominantly in secondary English and social studies classrooms. Steps in implementing the process are as follows:

1. Begin by raising a big question about the topic, one that is central to understanding it.
2. Have students complete a reading and an activity related to it.
3. Divide the class into two sections and reseat them in an inner or outer ring. (The inner-ring students respond directly to the discussion questions posed by the teacher, and the outer-ring students take notes on the discussion for comment later.)
4. Hold the discussion with inner-ring students, using questions and follow-up probes.
5. Assign an application activity as homework.
6. Hold the discussion with outer-ring students, using appropriate questions and probes.
7. Use a broad question to conclude the discussion with both groups, culminating in the sharing of samples of student work on the application activity.
8. Assess the individual homework samples and provide appropriate feedback.

Model Lesson 6: The Socratic Seminar

Instructional purpose:
- To explore personal decision-making processes (three class periods required)

Big questions:
- How important is decision making in today's world?
- How equipped do you feel to make prudent decisions in your life?

Activity: All students read a set of scenarios where a decision is called for. (One might be on making decisions about college, another about course taking, a third about peer pressure to participate in a questionable activity.) Students then work in small groups to reach decisions on each scenario, rotating to a new scenario every 15 minutes. A full discussion of the scenarios can be carried out over the next two class periods.

Discussion questions include:
- What processes did you employ to address the scenarios? *Probes:* Were they the same or different across the group of situations? Why do you think that was the case?
- What would happen if your decisions were implemented for each scenario? *Probes:* Are the outcomes appropriate in your view? Why or why not?
- How did the decisions you made affect other people in each scenario? *Probes:* Were the decisions moral and ethical in nature? In what ways?
- What criteria are important to consider in making real-world decisions? *Probe:* Why?
- Follow-up assignment: Describe in a two- to- three-page statement an important decision you have to make and how you will use the criteria we generated to make it (due the next class period).

Follow-up discussion with "observer" students:
- What key ideas did you hear in the discussion about the scenarios that you thought were important to emphasize further? (Facilitator probes each response.)

Model Lesson 6: The Socratic Seminar, continued.

- What three criteria from the discussion are the most critical in decision making in your opinion? *Probes:* Why these three? How did you apply them in your statement of personal decision making?
- What did you learn from observing the discussion yesterday as opposed to participating in it? *Probe:* Why did such learning occur for you as a passive observer?

Whole-class question: What do you now know to apply to personal decision making that you did not know before? Will these processes work for you in all situations? Why or why not?

Homework follow-up: Let's hear a few of the application statements you worked on last night. (Have three students read. Comments on each one may be solicited.)

Assessment: All statements are collected and read by the teacher. Feedback is posted electronically to each student. The statement is placed in a portfolio to be student-developed.

Note. Adapted from "Secondary Affective Curriculum and Instruction for Gifted Learners" by J. VanTassel-Baska, J. S. McIntosh, and K. L. Kearney, in *The Handbook of Secondary Gifted Education* (2nd ed., pp. 522–524), by F. A. Dixon and S. M. Moon (Eds.), 2015, Waco, TX: Prufrock Press. Copyright 2015 by Prufrock Press. Adapted with permission.

Tips for Teachers

The following practical suggestions for implementation provide teachers more ideas to use these archetypal lessons effectively.

General Tips
- ☑ Treat all knowledge as tentative (e.g., asking your students, "What do you think?" about an event or a process). This encourages students to question regularly based on your model.

☑ Articulate your own thinking or decision-making process to help students see another way of looking at questions. You then become a model for students to emulate in question-asking procedures.

Before the Lesson

☑ Preassess knowledge on the current topic or on questioning strategies as a whole.

☑ Group and possibly regroup students based on preassessment.

During the Lesson

☑ Allow sufficient thinking time for students to pose thoughtful questions and/or answers.

☑ Allow time for whole-group responses, small-group responses, and individual responses to prompts.

After the Lesson

☑ Include a postassessment on the current topic or questioning strategies, using the same or similar questions from the preassessment.

☑ Use exit tickets that allow students to share how their thinking process has changed.

☑ Consider future grouping based on ability within inquiry activities. For example, one inquiry activity might show that a student can work at a deeper level. This student could then be paired with a different partner or group in the future.

Creative Expression

Another complex form of problem solving that involves both critical and creative thinking is creative problem solving. This model is widely applied in gifted programs and special extracurricular programs, such as Odyssey of the Mind and Future Problem Solving Program International (Treffinger, Isaksen, & Dorval, 2000).

Six steps or processes characterize the model (Treffinger et. al, 2000):

1. **Mess finding:** Participants sort through a problem situation and find direction toward a broad goal or solution.
2. **Data finding:** Participants sort through all available information about the mess and clarify the steps or direction to a solution.
3. **Problem finding:** A specific problem statement is formulated.
4. **Idea finding:** Participants process many ideas for solutions to the problem or parts of the problem.
5. **Solution finding:** Participants use an evaluation process to sort through the ideas produced in the last step and select those most likely to produce solutions.
6. **Acceptance finding:** A plan is devised for implementing the good solution.

An adaptation of the creative problem solving model is called Future Problem Solving. It involves the application of the creative problem solving model to emerging problems and studies of the future.

Treffinger et al. (2000) extended the creative problem solving model by suggesting that the mess-finding stage should include opportunities for participants to identify their problem within a specific domain of interest or study. The solution-finding stage should also involve more than selecting best ideas; it should involve synthesizing the best ideas into a more complex and creative solution.

Parts of this model may be used to help students enhance creative expression. The following model lesson in economics exemplifies that well.

Model Lesson 7: Economics

Instructional purpose:
- To highlight the problem-solving approaches used to solve the financial crisis of 2008

Activities: Students should be organized into small groups of 4–5 for addressing the problem. The following stages of the process of problem solving should be followed. The teacher may act as a facilitator of the learning by rotating among groups to provide assistance as needed.

1. **Mess finding:** Investigate the financial crisis of 2008. Brainstorm its components.
2. **Data finding:** What resources can we locate to help us understand what the crisis was and how various stakeholders responded to it?
3. **Solution finding:** What was the process of solution finding used by our government to stave off financial disaster? What were the component parts of solutions needed?
4. **Plan of action:** How might you handle the continuing crisis of the financial industry? Develop a plan of action to resolve one aspect of the problem. To whom would you direct your ideas? Why?

Students conclude the lesson (after approximately 5 days) by presenting their plan of action for review by peers and teacher.

Assessment: Peers and teachers review the action plans.

A less developed use of the model may be seen in the following physics lesson where the teacher employs open-ended activities. Through this lesson, students can demonstrate their understanding of how to measure friction, design questions to be answered about the process, and indicate where to find resources for use in problem solving.

Model Lesson 8: Physics—Inclined Plane With Friction

Instructional purpose:
- To help students become proficient at:
  - free body diagramming on an inclined plane,
  - determining the coefficient of static friction of a block initially at rest on an incline, and
  - determining the coefficient of kinetic friction using the acceleration of the block as it slides down the ramp.

Activities:
1. Draw a free body diagram of the wooden block as it sits motionless on the ramp.
2. Use this free body diagram to determine a relationship between the coefficient of static friction and the angle of elevation of the ramp.
3. What is the coefficient of static friction between your block and ramp?
4. What do you need to know, in addition to the physics formulas provided, in order to solve for this coefficient?
5. How will you go about finding out?

Assessment: Assess product diagrams via a rubric.

Tips for Teachers

The following practical suggestions for implementation provide teachers more ideas to use these archetypal lessons effectively.

- ☑ Be sure to ask open-ended questions as students navigate these activities. Do not provide answers for students.
- ☑ Encourage multiple right answers from students in order to create an atmosphere of open acceptance of all ideas. Do not let students believe you are looking for one right answer.
- ☑ Discuss with students how real-world problem solving employs creative open-endedness to solve problems.
- ☑ Remind students of the rules of brainstorming so that all have a voice, can express their ideas orally, and record and accept all ideas.
- ☑ Monitor the process carefully to avoid expressing praise or disapproval of student ideas.

The Arts as a Cognitive Tool for Learning

Using the arts in classrooms that contain students with special needs provides an intellectual and affective focus for their thinking (VanTassel-Baska, Buckingham, & Baska, 2009). For example, students can study a myth, examine art pieces that depict the characters or situations in the myth, and then describe how the artistic rendering helps provide greater clarity in respect to the meaning of the myth. Use of the visual arts is especially effective with ELLs who benefit from having the visual stimulus, which they can connect to content studied and use as a basis for discussing culture and values. This approach is also very effective with twice-exceptional students who may prefer visual modes of learning to auditory ones.

Any area of study can benefit from connection to the arts, but the following model lessons exemplify two ways to connect classroom content to the arts for the benefit of ELLs and other gifted learners with special needs.

Model Lesson 9: Viewing Artistic Objects

Instructional purpose:
- To introduce students to ways of viewing artistic media

Activities:
- Analyze a selected poem, art object, and musical work (e.g., songs, instrumental pieces).
- Answer the following questions about each. Then answer how they are all similar.
    1. What is the theme or major ideas of the work?
    2. What mood does the work convey?
    3. How is the work organized? What is its structure?
    4. How would you describe the form of the work?
    5. What is the purpose of the work?
    6. What are aspects of the work that you most enjoy? Why?

- Write a critical review of a play, movie, or other performance (e.g., analyze the performance via characterizations, storyline, and theme expressed).

93

Model Lesson 9: Viewing Artistic Objects, continued.

- Design relevant objet d'art, using key design specifications, such as rhythm, tone, color, theme, subject matter, perspective, symmetry/balance, and variety.

Assessment: Use the criteria for design to assess student products created. Narrative comment on each criterion should be provided.

Note. Adapted from "Curriculum Development for Low-Income and Minority Gifted Learners" by J. VanTassel-Baska, in *Patterns and Profiles of Promising Learners From Poverty* (p. 209), by J. VanTassel-Baska (Ed.), 2010, Waco, TX: Prufrock Press. Copyright 2010 by National Association for Gifted Children. Adapted with permission.

The following lesson on the arts asks students to consider the same situation, based on a common myth, rendered in a painting and a poem. The interdisciplinary thinking required for students to engage in this lesson is at a high level and diversified in type, as questions require cross-analysis of multiple art forms.

Model Lesson 10: Use of the Arts

Instructional Purpose:
- To connect mythology to artistic representations in poetry and visual arts.

Activities:
1. Ask students to read a version of the Daedalus and Icarus myth from an online source or from Edith Hamilton or Thomas Bulfinch mythology books.
2. Discuss the following questions about the myth with the whole class.
   - Why did ancient people need a myth like this one?
   - What purposes did this story fulfill? What was its moral for the Greeks and Romans?
   - What pattern does the myth follow?

Model Lesson 10: Use of the Arts, continued.

- ◆ What aspects of human behavior does the myth demonstrate?
- ◆ Icarus tries out the wings that his father Daedalus created, which are eventually responsible for his demise. What aspects of being creative or innovative are being explored here? What lessons are learned?
- ◆ What lessons are revealed about fathers and sons?

3. Have students read the William Carlos Williams poem about the painting by Pieter Bruegel entitled "Landscape with the Fall of Icarus." While they are reading the poem, project the painting on screen for them to view.

4. In small groups, have students analyze the painting and the poem in relationship to the myth. Ask the following questions regarding the painting.
- ◆ What do you see in the painting that relates to the myth?
- ◆ What important ideas from the myth are portrayed?
- ◆ What images and symbols does Bruegel employ?
- ◆ What is the structure of the painting? How is it organized?
- ◆ What feelings does the painting produce in you as the viewer?

5. Ask the following questions regarding the poem.
- ◆ What words are important in conveying the tone of the poem?
- ◆ What images that Williams uses are the most powerful? Why?
- ◆ What is the theme of this poem?
- ◆ How do you react to the poem?
- ◆ What structural devices does Williams use to heighten the impact of his poem?

6. Ask the following questions regarding the comparison of myth, picture, and poem.
- ◆ How do Williams and Bruegel each interpret the myth? Are there distinctions in their interpretation?
- ◆ How does each artist extend the myth for the audience of their time?

Model Lesson 10: Use of the Arts, continued.

◆ Both the writer and the painter were working in innovative forms in their art when they did these works. What aspects of creativity do you see in each product? Read about Bruegel and Williams in respect to their work.

Follow-up project: Have students select a Roman myth of their choice and create a poem and illustration that depicts that myth. Have them write an artist's statement about key aspects of interpretation (i.e., theme, vocabulary, structure, images, and symbols). Student products should be judged according to the following criteria:

- Interpretation of the myth selected in both words and images
- Quality of the products
- Use of creative and innovative ideas
- Use of effective images in both the poem and the illustration
- Effective discussion of artistic elements employed
- Command of language mechanics (i.e., spelling, grammar, and usage)

Note. Adapted from *Ancient Roots and Ruins: A Guide to Understanding the Romans, Their World, and Their Language* (pp. 180–183), by A. Baska and J. VanTassel-Baska, 2014, Waco, TX: Prufrock Press. Copyright 2014 by Prufrock Press. Adapted with permission.

Tips for Teachers

The following practical suggestions for implementation provide teachers more ideas to use these archetypal lessons effectively.

Visual Arts

☑ Analysis of visuals works best if each student group has its own copy of the artwork in question (laminated color photocopies work best, if your school has the resources).

☑ Before beginning the lesson, give students time to think about and discuss what they see in the picture. They could brainstorm with ability groups or independently.

☑ Provide sticky notes that allow students to comment on or label the picture with ideas or questions during their discussion.

Poetry

☑ Analysis of poetry works best if each student has his or her own copy to mark up with questions and ideas.

☑ Marking up unfamiliar or interesting vocabulary and images helps special needs populations, particularly English language learners.

☑ If there is time, use the Literature Web model (see Appendix A), which can help all learners evaluate a work.

Performance/Drama

☑ All video clips incorporated into the curriculum should be subtitled for the benefit of both English language learners and any deaf or hard of hearing students.

☑ All audio clips (dramatic readings, etc.) should be played multiple times for all students.

☑ Make sure students are evaluating the content and the performance aspects of the clip separately.

Music

☑ Select in advance a key set of characteristics that you want your students to listen for, so that they can listen with purpose.

☑ If the music has lyrics, each student should receive a copy of those lyrics. If the lyrics are in a second language, the original language text should be provided with a translation.

☑ Play audio clips at least twice for all students.

General

☑ Whole-group discussion of first questions about the text can model how discussion within small groups should happen.

☑ Small groups can report observations and reflections on content during a whole-group wrap-up.

☑ Allow students to share final thoughts orally or write on a chart. This gives choice to students who have anxiety about their writing or speaking abilities.

Affective Curriculum Needs

Interventions for gifted students with special needs must also consider areas beyond what the student case studies have suggested. Most of the case studies mentioned the importance of clinical personnel in student development, so it is important to consider what clinical applications might be used in the classroom to motivate students to perform at high levels (Peterson, 2009). Developing activities that promote student understanding of who they are, what they are interested in, and what they care about aids student motivation to achieve (Siegle & McCoach, 2005). Several approaches may be employed to accomplish these ends: bibliotherapy, videotherapy, discussion groups, and lessons designed on the principles of emotional intelligence. Figure 5 shows these four approaches to meeting the affective needs of gifted learners with special needs. One of the easiest approaches to implement may be bibliotherapy.

Bibliotherapy

The use of books in addressing the affective concerns of gifted learners has long been lauded as an intervention by itself, but it is magnified in effectiveness when the books reflect the specific issues of special needs populations (Halsted, 2009). Bibliotherapy, then, can be useful in helping students explore issues of identity development (Frank & McBee, 2003), emotional intelligence (Sullivan & Strang, 2002), and multiculturalism (Ford, 2013), among other issues.

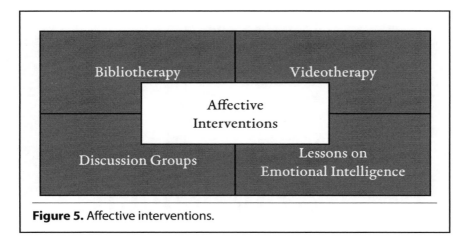

Figure 5. Affective interventions.

Specific genres of literature can be useful for helping students come to grips with different kinds of social and emotional issues. The reading of biography, for example, can provide role models for students to emulate, people who have encountered the same issues they are experiencing. Biographies of individuals who grew up poor but were successful can help a child in poverty have hope for a more positive future, and biographies of people with disabilities can help a child see that a disability need not hold him or her back from developing abilities. The reading of poetry that is representative of one's culture can have an elevating effect on mood and provide powerful images for students to consider about their heritage and ways that it helps define who they are. Myths, stories, and fables further provide a strong tie to various cultures with which students may identify.

The *Jacob's Ladder Reading Comprehension Program* was written in response to teachers' findings that students in Title I classrooms needed additional scaffolding to work consistently at higher levels of thinking in reading (see VanTassel-Baska & Stambaugh, 2006). The new *Affective Jacob's Ladder Reading Comprehension Program* (VanTassel-Baska & Stambaugh, 2018) is designed to develop both cognitive and affective areas through the use of instructional scaffolds, which have been found to enhance reading comprehension skills. The new affective ladders stress emotional intelligence, coping with adversity, identity development, risk-taking, managing stress, achievement motivation, and developing excellence. They are used to encourage students to discuss poetry, short stories, videos, and biographical selections.

The following model lesson is taken from a unit on emotional intelligence and identity, which requires students to read selected text and then respond to that text through questions for discussion and activities that promote deeper thinking and feeling. To promote multicultural understanding, the selections below represent poetry from African American poets Georgia Johnson and Claude McKay.

Model Lesson 11: Bibliotherapy

Instructional purposes:
- To expose students to affective language
- To address identity issues

Activities: Students should read the poetry of both Georgia Johnson and Claude McKay. If they read at least 3–4 poems from each writer, that should be sufficient to address the questions below. The poem "Comrades Four" by McKay should be read to do the second set of activities.

Identity development:
1. "Who am I?" is a central question we all ask at different times in our lives. What would be the poet's answer? Would you give a similar or different answer to the question? Why?
2. The poet feels like the product of disparate ancestors. What is your ancestral heritage? How does that impact your thinking about who you are?
3. Develop an essay that describes your sense of self in contrary terms as seen in the poetry (e.g., I am this, not that . . .). Now summarize what you learned about yourself from doing this exercise.

Ask students to read African American poet Claude McKay's poem "Comrades Four" and discuss the role of emotional words in making it effective.

Using the language of emotion:
1. The poem speaks of the narrator passing "through the open door" and "fleeing from the life of gall." To what is he referring in these lines? How does the transition implied in these lines affect our reading of the poem?
2. The theme of "solidarity" is central to understanding the poem. What words does McKay use to convey that idea?
3. Create a poem of your own, using the word *comrades* as a central image. Make it at least three stanzas of four lines each, with an ABCB rhyme scheme, after McKay. Choose words that evoke emotion to tell the story.

Model Lesson 11: Bibliotherapy, continued.

Assessment: Assess the product created in question 3 of both sets of questions (i.e., an essay and a poem), using the criteria of organization, content, and adherence to the demands of the assignment. A narrative should be developed to critique each of these criteria.

Note. Adapted from *Affective Jacob's Ladder Reading Comprehension Program (Grades 4–5)*, by J. VanTassel-Baska and T. Stambaugh, 2018, Waco, TX: Prufrock Press. Copyright 2018 by Prufrock Press. Adapted with permission.

Videotherapy

Just as books can play an important role in the social-emotional development of gifted children from special populations, so too can films that feature gifted students in similarly adverse circumstances. The following page provides a list of films organized by special populations of the gifted. Although all of these films can benefit student understanding of giftedness in some way, they are most beneficial in helping students understand special populations in particular. These films are provided with running time, to allow for effective planning of pre-film and post-film discussions. Recommended age ranges are also included as a guideline, based on ratings and content. Gifted students, however, may be ready for films at earlier ages and benefit significantly from the discussions sparked by these films at earlier stages of learning.

The following are general questions that could be used with these, or other, films. Questions can be made more specific if the teacher desires.

1. What are the traits of the central character that reveal his or her abilities?
2. What obstacles does the central character face, and how does he or she overcome them?
3. What family relationships are depicted in the film? What family influences help or hinder the development of the gifted character or characters? In what way does this occur?
4. What role do people outside the family play in promoting the development of the central character (e.g., teachers, mentors, etc.)?
5. What were the accomplishments of the central character (if applicable), and how were they possible?
6. How effectively did the film portray gifted learners with special needs? What criteria did you use to judge this?

General Recommendations

The Incredibles (2004)
Length: 1 hr 55 min.
Recommended Ages: 7+

Although this film doesn't address special populations of the gifted per se, the problems of trying to fit in despite differences are addressed in different ways throughout the film. The writers deliberately create many parallels between superpowers and giftedness in a film that will appeal equally to a wide range of ages.

Inside Out (2015)
Length: 1 hr 35 min.
Recommended Ages: 8+

This film is highly recommended to address social-emotional needs in gifted students, particularly those facing emotional disturbance, depression, and anxiety disorders. In animated form, it presents emotions as characters, allowing the viewer to see characteristics and interactions up close. The film is a wonderful tool for allowing students to think about their own cognitive and emotional processes.

Spellbound (2002)
Length: 1 hr 37 min.
Recommended Ages: 10+

This documentary follows a group of students as they prepare for the National Spelling Bee. The students from various backgrounds vie for a title that means different things to each of them. The film does a wonderful job of exploring cultural definitions of success, while at the same time honoring who each of these children are. Students of poverty, twice-exceptional students, and English language learners are all portrayed, competing to see who will win the title.

The Point (1971)
Length: 1hr 14 min.
Recommended Ages: 5+

This fantastical film is highly recommended for students who look different or think differently from their peers. This film examines how society deals with differences in a more conceptual way, as the round-headed Oblio and his dog Arrow are exiled from the pointy world in which they live. Oblio and Arrow wander through a nonsensical land of wonders and wordplay (not unlike Alice's Wonderland). Recommended mostly for younger students.

Twice-Exceptional and Learning Disabilities

Temple Grandin (2010)
Length: 1 hr 48 min.
Recommended Ages: 14+

This biopic presents the life of Temple Grandin, a noted author and advocate for accommodations for students with ASD. The film traces her development, particularly focusing on her time at a boarding school, where she learned to take care of animals, and the slaughterhouse where she developed a more humane way to treat the animals. Given the nature of the slaughterhouse scenes, this film is only recommended for students at the secondary level, although segments from the film can be shown to students at earlier stages of learning.

Life Animated (2016)
Length: 1 hr 31 min.
Recommended Ages: 9+

This documentary centers on the story of a boy with ASD who uses Disney films to process emotions and relationships. The film features many Disney film clips with discussion of how he views each scene, making explicit his cognitive and emotional connections to each movie. The film also discusses many important topics, from bullying, to the meaning of independence, to the ways that people connect to each other.

Finding Nemo (2003)
Length: 1 hr 40 min.
Recommended Ages: 5+

This film features so many characters with different kinds of disabilities, that it is ideal for a wide array of twice-exceptional students. The central character, Nemo, has a stunted fin that challenges his mobility, but the film also features characters with post-traumatic stress disorder, anxiety disorders, memory loss, addiction, and obsessive-compulsive disorder. Almost every character in this film faces some kind of challenge, and although the simple storyline focuses on a father's search for his son, few other films focus on acceptance of self and others so effectively.

Itzhak (2017)
Length: 1 hr 22 min.
Recommended Ages: 10+

This film traces the career of Itzhak Perlman, the world-renowned violinist who overcame the effects of childhood polio to develop his considerable musical talent, first in Israel and then in the U.S. at Juilliard School in New York, NY. Upbeat and humorous throughout, this film depicts Perlman's unique evolution as a versatile violinist.

Poverty

Queen of Katwe (2016)
Length: 2 hr 4 min.
Recommended Ages: 9+

Based on the true story of a young girl from Uganda, this film focuses on her life from the moment she is first introduced to chess. Competitions with wealthier schools, districts, and countries follow, but the film is not a typical underdog story. The girl's internal conflict and the conflict between her equally important family life and her education will make for particularly interesting discussion.

Akeelah and the Bee (2006)
Length: 1 hr 52 min.
Recommended Ages: 11+

This film spins the story of a young, intelligent, but underachieving girl from south Los Angeles who happens upon her school's spelling bee as a way to avoid detention. When she wins, her principal pairs her with a tutor to prepare her for the regional spelling bee. All of the main characters in this film are minorities, and the impediments to success for characters from poverty and minority backgrounds are portrayed clearly.

Kes (1969)
Length: 1 hr 50 min.
Recommended ages: 14+

This film revolves around the life of a young boy, bullied at home and school. Billy Casper, a 15-year-old boy from a working-class mining town in Yorkshire, finds an escape from his circumstances in learning to train and care for a pet kestrel falcon. With only the encouragement of his English teacher and a few classmates, he finds a purpose in his life. Although this film is brilliantly written and directed, the grim setting will be off-putting to some viewers, as will the disturbing story elements that emerge near the end. Be warned: This film does not have a happy ending, although it is the most critically acclaimed film on this list.

English Language Learners

The Future Perfect (2016)
Length: 1 hr 5 min.
Recommended ages: 10+

This film tells the story of a teenage girl, Xiaobei, a recent émigré from China to Argentina, as she tries to learn Spanish to work in a grocery store in Buenos Aires. The film very explicitly details the process of Xiaobei's second language learning, with textbook dialogue about vocabulary and grammar concepts. Xiaobei's story is engaging, too, as she goes on dates with Vijay, a young immigrant from India. This film describes the reality of the immigrant experience and shows sensitivity to language, and how it empowers people.

Stranger Than Paradise (1984)
Length: 1 hr 29 min.
Recommended Ages: 15+

This unusual black-and-white film captures a different side of the immigrant experience through the lens of Eva, a Hungarian immigrant who goes to live with her hipster cousin Willie in New York. Conflict ensues as Willie expects Eva to reject everything about her home country and language to fit in with his American friends. The film contains some profanity, smoking, and drinking, particularly as Eva tries to create a new image for herself.

Discussion Groups

Peterson (2009) suggested the need to hold ongoing discussions with gifted learners about their concerns. Top concerns of secondary gifted learners tend to focus on developing relationships, perfectionism, and dealing with criticism. Educators can organize small groups of 10–12 students to discuss a film or book, using guided questions that allow students to study the behavior of characters. This character study can help them develop an understanding of and sensitivity to the concerns of others as well.

Model Lesson 12: Discussion Groups

Instructional purpose:
To create a forum for students to discuss social and emotional issues, using books and/or films as the stimulus for the discussion

---

Model Lesson 12: Discussion Groups, continued.

Activities: The following questions may be applied to such discussions in order to elicit lively responses from gifted learners with special needs:

1. Make a list of words that come to mind to describe your over-all reactions to the book or film. (Ask a few students to share their list and rationalize the choices.)
2. What kinds of relationships were presented in the book or film? Were they healthy, unhealthy or mixed? Defend your opinion.
3. What character in the book or movie did you most identify with and why?
4. Did the main characters change their attitudes throughout the book/movie? If so, how and why?
5. Share with a partner what you liked the most and did not like at all about the book/movie. Provide examples to support your preferences. (Ask a few students to share their views, and then ask students to disagree with their peers' perspectives, presenting counterexamples.)

Conclude the discussion by asking students to do a 10-minute journal entry on how they benefited from the discussion. Now discuss as a whole group the importance of hearing others' perspectives, especially if they are different from yours.

Assessment: Teachers may want to create videos of selected discussions and critique the quality of the discussion, the number of students responding to the questions, and the nature of student interactions during the discussion. A review of journal entries may also be useful to determine individual student perceptions of benefit.

Emotional Intelligence

In addition to understanding their emotions and the emotions of others, students need to learn how to perceive their emotional reactions. The way that students interpret speeches and reports from media sources around them can influence their ideas and opinions without them realizing the effect on their feelings. Giving students time to focus on the emotional content of these data streams allows them to evaluate their world.

Model Lesson 13: Emotional Intelligence

Instructional purpose: To allow students to apply emotional understanding to cognitive tasks, giving them the tools to analyze and evaluate emotional triggers around them

Activities:

1. Give students a copy of a famous speech from history (e.g., The Gettysburg Address, John F. Kennedy's Inaugural Address, Martin Luther King, Jr.'s "I Have a Dream" speech).

2. Have students highlight words that generate emotions, either for them, or that they would expect to trigger emotions in others.

3. Have students highlight repeated words or phrases.

4. Ask students to discuss in seminar style the emotional content of the speech's language.

5. If possible, play students an audio or video clip of the speech.

6. Have students discuss the following questions:

    ◆ Did your perception of the emotions of the speaker change based on the performance of the speech compared to the text?

    ◆ How would you expect an audience member on the day this speech was given to react?

    ◆ Are there different emotions presented in this speech? If so, how are they related?

    ◆ What are the causes and consequences of these feelings, both short-term and long-term?

    ◆ Are there complex or contradictory feelings expressed in this speech? Historically, how did the audience react to these feelings?

    ◆ Could the audience have reacted to this speech differently? Explain how that might have happened and why.

    ◆ How would you react to this speech as an audience member? What would you do as a reaction to the emotions stirred up by the speech?

Model Lesson 13: Emotional Intelligence, continued.

Product: Have students write a journal entry, answering the following prompt: *How has this activity changed your opinion about how emotions are used in writing and speeches? How has this activity changed your opinion on how emotions may have shaped history?*

Assessment: Review journal entries, using the criteria of content and organization of thinking.

Tips for Teachers

The following practical suggestions for implementation provide teachers more ideas to use these archetypal lessons effectively.

- ☑ Carefully select books and movies for major themes, issues, and affective concerns portrayed. It is also important to consider appropriate developmental issues, cultural stereotyping, and language use.
- ☑ Books should be vetted by school librarians before use. You will, of course, still need to preview all material to be used and create additional activities and questions as needed.
- ☑ Discuss your plans for these lessons with the school counseling office and invite a representative to participate. Because sensitive issues may arise from these discussions, having counseling resources on hand may be helpful.
- ☑ Relate content to students in a modern context. Questions such as "How do these ideas relate to us today?" and "How do attitudes portrayed seem similar or dissimilar to attitudes today?" can help students connect with the material.
- ☑ Encourage multiple perspectives to be raised in the discussion so that all students can share their ideas, regardless of background.
- ☑ Have an exit ticket for students to write down an alternative title for the work, based on their new understanding from the discussion of the work.

Conclusion

The interventions described in Part II of this text directly respond to students' own reflections on what worked well for them in school, based on this book's research. These interventions represent archetypal activities for use with these learners in differing subject areas and levels of learning. Students not only identified these strategies as the most effective, but also credited them, in some instances, with their success throughout their years of schooling. Interventions can be very effective for these students, as their stories have attested, but without established structures to support them, many students flounder. The next section discusses in depth the need for advocacy and collaboration, as well as suggestions for how professionals can put in place meaningful support systems for these special needs students.

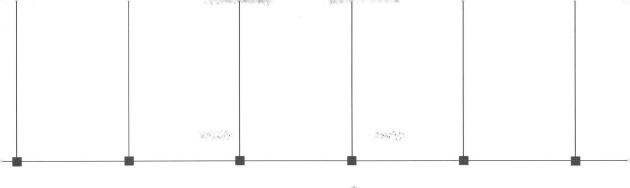

PART III

Support Structures for Intervention Services

Learning is not attained by chance, it must be sought for with ardour and attended to with diligence.

—Abigail Adams

As shown by the case studies in Part I, many issues surround the provision of appropriate services to these special populations of learners. For these students to succeed to their full potential, these issues need to be acknowledged and addressed. As shown with the identified interventions in Part II, strategies exist to support the needs of these learners in the classroom and beyond. Yet all of the interventions listed, although helpful to student learning, rely on stakeholders who understand the role they have to play in effecting change in these students' lives. This section discusses how teachers, parents, administrators, counselors, and clinicians can work together to support these students.

Developing Support Structures for Special Populations

The integration of support structures will undoubtedly benefit gifted students, ensuring a network of professionals connected to each other and committed to student needs. Schools and individuals can begin this process by encouraging teachers, administrators, counselors, and clinicians to engage and collaborate with each other. For this process, time devoted to communication about these students as individuals is essential. In addition, involving other professionals who have expertise in areas of specialization whenever possible is key. Gaining more understanding about these students from sociocultural and psychological perspectives will be important to understanding how best to serve them. For the field of gifted education to progress, teachers, administrators, and counselors need to engage and collaborate with each other and with professionals from other relevant disciplines in working with special populations.

The choice of school program delivery systems is also crucial in developing a framework of support. As the need to understand both individual and group differences among gifted learners becomes greater, resource capacity becomes more limited, and schools are forced to rely on existing organizational structures to deliver curriculum services. Consequently, the U.S. is experiencing a movement to provide for gifted learners in the regular classroom at a time when educational budgets are shrinking. The push toward cooperative teaching strategies and away from pull-out programs that use a resource teacher to work directly with small groups of gifted learners is common among districts nationwide. Although instructional grouping and regrouping is the hallmark of effective teaching, separate and distinct grouping of gifted learners is less likely to occur under this model. Although it is counterintuitive, grouping special populations of gifted learners together is likely to enhance their growth and development, rather than using patchy approaches that do not allow sustained periods of intervention to occur across years.

Educators must also acknowledge the importance of working with these learners over time in a well-developed curriculum that allows authentic growth to take place. Too often, teachers give up, believing that a student is not capable of higher level thinking at a stage of development, rather than persisting in using high-level material. Several studies have documented that persistent use of high-level scaffolds, when given across multiple years, yields increased identification of special populations of gifted learners, (VanTassel-Baska, Feng, & de Brux, 2007; VanTassel-Baska, Johnson, & Avery, 2002).

The Role of Advocacy to Ensure Intervention Services

All school personnel may need to advocate for these gifted learners with special needs. Each of these students stands to benefit from a network of support, or at least several adults in their lives who care about them and their future. Table 3 has been developed to share intervention ideas for advocacy that might be activated by different groups in the school.

Often well-intentioned educators have great difficulty planning for the needs of exceptional gifted learners due to common misconceptions that can be deeply held by teachers, administrators, counselors, and other support staff within a school. Most misconceptions about these learners can be grouped into two categories: (1) misconceptions that would lead teachers to exclude students with special needs from the gifted program and (2) misconceptions that prevent best teaching practice for this population.

A reproducible guide is provided (see p. 118) as a resource to help with the advocacy process and debunk commonly held tenets about both gifted students and students with special needs.

Although misconceptions about special needs populations may overshadow their chances of being identified for gifted programs, the real concern lies with ensuring that their educational program is sound and well-taught by teachers who understand their needs. The next section examines the characteristics of teachers who have been successful with these students in general education classrooms, as well as specialized programs for the gifted.

Table 3

Advocacy Interventions

Role	Approaches to Advocacy
Administrators	• Provide resources to teachers • Provide time for collaboration between teachers, counselors, and clinicians about individual student needs • Offer cross-categorical identification workshops to teachers and other professionals in the building • Educate parents through e-mails about available school resources
Psychologists/social workers/clinicians	• Provide resources to teachers • Provide time for collaboration between teachers, counselors, and clinicians about individual student needs • Offer cross-categorical identification workshops to teachers and other professionals in the building • Educate parents through e-mails about available school resources

Common Misconceptions About Gifted Learners With Special Needs

1. A student's education should focus on areas of weakness first.

There is a tendency to focus on areas of weakness in a student's profile, and to use those data as evidence for the student not being able to handle advanced programs.

These students often are not discerned as gifted by school staff, who might refuse to see beyond one label. Many teachers have difficulty recognizing characteristics different from the ones they're looking for, based on a student's profile. For example, a teacher may focus on bad handwriting or poor spelling as a reason not to assign advanced work to students with special needs. A teacher may also cite disruptive behavior as a basis for withholding advanced work.

2. Gifted students should be equally strong in all areas.

Students are perceived as weak when a strength area is hidden and weaknesses are evident.

Many students with special needs have only one area of giftedness and many weaknesses, rather than only one area of weakness and many gifts, found in more typical gifted learners. For example, a student may be strong in handling derivatives in math, an advanced concept, but limited in respect to discussion in class, a more common criterion for judging giftedness. Unevenness in skills is the norm, not the exception. A teacher should expect gaps in knowledge and skill sets in these students and be prepared to provide the additional instruction necessary, rather than use these gaps against students for purposes of placement in gifted programs and classes.

3. Gifted student behaviors look the same from all cultures.

Sociocultural norms are often held against students from other cultures.

For some students from minority backgrounds, their culture may dictate specific behavioral characteristics. For example, if they are female, cultural gender expectations may dictate maintaining silence in the face of challenge. In other cultures, active talk and conversation may be the norm. Neither of these outcomes may be perceived as desirable traits in certain academic settings. In some classrooms, active talk may be discouraged because a quiet, focused environment is the norm. In other classrooms, passive listening may be discouraged because lively debate is the norm. These differences can impact how students from other cultures are perceived in their readiness to learn and their capacity to do so at advanced levels.

4. **All gifted students learn in similar ways.**

   Educators may ignore the range of gifted personality behaviors and use particular observed behaviors as a reason to include or exclude students from gifted programs.

   Behaviors such as choosing to work alone or resisting small-group work may lead to students not being considered for gifted programs that are dependent on small-group work—with little consideration for individual interests or preferences for work style.

5. **Gifted students follow all procedures well.**

   Procedures and mechanics of learning should not be used as criteria for judging who is gifted.

   Basic procedural and mechanical skill sets are not primary determiners of student giftedness. Students who have difficulty with spelling or organization may still be gifted conceptually even though mechanical mistakes may be rampant. Such problems alone should not preclude identification.

6. **Gifted students are mature in all respects.**

   Social-emotional development is often used as a proxy for readiness to learn.

   Students may often be excluded from being identified, based on social or emotional maturity factors. For example, students who do not work well with other students in the classroom may be left out of a project-based learning program for the gifted because teachers feel they would be too difficult to fit into an organizational plan for group learning. Students who don't have the maturity to control their emotions can often appear defiant in the classroom, which, for many teachers, automatically removes them from consideration for advanced learning opportunities.

7. **Only students identified as gifted should receive advanced work.**

   Teaching advanced skills and concepts needs to be a prelude to identification so that students can show advanced reasoning power.

   If students are only given basic skill level work on a mastery model, many will never show their true capabilities. In individual psychological assessments, for example, a student is given three opportunities to attempt more difficult material, yet in classrooms they often only get one chance if they miss an item at a given level. Moreover, the concept on which the skill is based may not be discussed such that a student can demonstrate a deeper understanding, or the assessment may be based on only the single problem being attempted.

8. The best intervention for gifted learners with special needs is group work.

Group work should not be the intervention of choice for working with gifted learners, as navigating the social skills required for group projects can be intimidating and difficult.

Many times, a student who is twice-exceptional may be perfectly capable intellectually of handling the assignments in group work but may be unable to handle working with others in the group due to anxiety or socialization issues. Many students with emotional disturbance or ASD face difficulties that preclude the ability to smoothly transition into group settings or perform well in social situations.

9. Learners with special needs can't handle acceleration.

Acceleration is too often viewed as something outside the reach of gifted learners with special needs, when it should be a regular part of their curriculum diet in their area or areas of strength.

Students with special needs can handle advanced curriculum and instruction in their content area of strength when given the opportunity through a special grouped advanced class, a short-term advanced offering, such as a summer class, or through tutorials. Thus, content-based acceleration is an important approach to employ with these learners. This may include providing an advanced STEM offering during the elementary years for students from poverty, or early entrance into foreign language classes at the middle school level.

10. Gifted learners with special needs can achieve only so much.

Gifted learners with special needs are more often underestimated than overestimated in terms of what they can do, whereas more typical gifted learners are more often overestimated.

Because of disabilities or special circumstances, learners with special needs are often perceived as lacking the qualities necessary to function well within a gifted program. Because the disability or circumstance may be easier to see, such as poverty or learning a second language, educators tend to notice first what a student cannot do rather than what he or she can do.

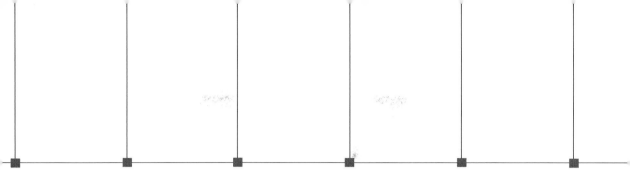

Characteristics and Practices of Successful Teachers

Teachers who work with special populations need to be trained to see both the gifts and the unique needs of these students. A teacher trained in gifted education will have 12 hours of endorsement coursework from an educational institution, including a practicum in which he or she is supervised in his or her work with these students in schools. This coursework should prepare the teacher to understand the characteristics of gifted learners, their needs, and how to meet those needs through cognitive and affective strategies. The teacher also should understand the dynamics of identification and programming for these students across the K–12 spectrum. It is expected that ongoing professional development will further hone his or her skills in addressing issues and problems of working with gifted students.

Training in specialized areas, particularly special education, working with English language learners, and working with students of poverty, is more challenging to arrange. Because teachers may receive education on one or more of these issues solely through limited workshops, teachers may feel unqualified in their attempts to address such needs. School districts, however, often as a part of their School Improvement Plans, offer professional development opportunities specifically focused on these unique populations, such as ELLs or special education students. The greatest determiners of readiness to work with children of poverty and those with cross-categorical disabilities may be empathy and openness to experiment with what interventions might work with such students. It is always wise, however, for teachers to consult professionals with greater expertise in the target area of need to ensure that they "first do no harm."

One of the graduates from the case studies commented:

> As I reflect on what influenced me, it was often . . . the teachers I had who were successful in encouraging and helping me develop skills and processes as a student. These teachers possessed specific qualities as people that promoted my growth in motivation and interest as a learner.

In addition to interventions, students in the case studies discussed teacher traits that helped them or hurt them in their development. The students had much to say about undesirable teacher traits, such as rigidity in thinking and classroom structures or emphasis on mechanics over concepts. The qualities described as most beneficial, however, were the ones associated with openness. "Open" teachers who were willing to try different approaches were described as "the most successful and influential teachers." Other positives identified in role model teachers were the use of metacognition to develop self-awareness in learners and the use of connected learning that provided interdisciplinary connections of interest (VanTassel-Baska & Little, 2017). These teachers were also cognizant of accommodations that would work well with twice-exceptional students.

Openness

Perhaps the most important teacher characteristic discussed in the case studies was the quality of openness. As one student expressed it,

> I valued the ability of a teacher to take the time to learn about me as a learner, and accept me on my own terms. . . . These teachers accepted the many ways in which I was different from my peers, and, rather than forcing me to conform to other ways of thinking and doing, they helped me explore learning in my own idiosyncratic way.

Another student shared an anecdote about learning to read and the influence of her teacher's guidance:

> In kindergarten, the primary focus was on reading. For years, I had been "performing books" but not reading them. I was quite talented at memorizing what to say with what inflection and when to turn the page. My talent was telling stories or performing them, rather than reading, which the reading specialist who visited our classroom three times a week did not like. The reading specialist believed in phonics. One day, she

demanded my attention in the middle of a lesson on phonics, but my hero of a teacher pulled me aside and indicated I was very close to working it out on my own, and she continued to work with me holistically, letting me mimic and write and tell stories. I wish I could remember precisely what she did that brought it all together for me, or that I could recall that "Eureka" moment of discovery when suddenly characters on the page became thoughts in my head. Sadly, I can't. I can say that through her openness to my experimentation with language, she allowed me to unlock the ability to read by January of that school year, and excused me from a system which made no sense to me, rather than forcing it upon me.

This student shared another memory from later years:

I also think of middle school where I had a drama teacher in eighth grade who, like the kindergarten teacher, warmly welcomed me into the world of performance. I was already obsessed with theatre from my exposure to great plays and musicals. I knew I had physical limitations related to my visual and auditory impairments, on top of my lack of coordination, but I wanted nothing more than to be on the stage. . . . She didn't wait for me to overcome my shyness or insist that I needed more training before receiving challenges with added responsibility. She met me where I was and helped me learn by doing. She was open to my abilities and my experiences, even if they didn't always match her expectations.

Use of Metacognitive Strategies

One of the most important instructional strategies used with these students was metacognition. Teachers who helped students to think about and discuss their own thinking were also regarded as highly successful. One student noted:

I had problems with math from an early age, often related to my visual problems—lining up columns of numbers for addition or subtraction was always an issue for me. I could not clearly articulate what was going wrong in my own head when I thought about mathematics and individual word problems, and I never felt as if I had the vocabulary to express my frustration when teachers wrote on my paper, again and again, "show your work." In elementary school, a family friend tutored me in math, and she was the first person to ask me to clearly articulate what I was thinking and the how and the

why of it. I had never heard of anyone caring how I was thinking about any subject before, most especially not math. I had
always gotten the impression in school that there was only
one way to do it. Anything else and your numbers would be
wrong. She put me on the spot every time we met, asking me
to tell her how I was learning the processes in school and how
I was thinking about them on my own. She tried getting me
to think through conceptual problems differently, visually, or
with manipulatives, like blocks or toothpicks, then asking me
to reflect on what was most effective for me.

This student provided another example from her high school years:

In a summer enrichment program, I took a condensed Advanced Placement Language and Composition class before
my sophomore year of high school. My teacher in this class
focused most strongly on clarity of thinking before clarity of
writing. He introduced me to the works of the great philos-
ophers—Plato, Aristotle, Descartes, Hegel, Marx, Wittgenstein
and the like. He wanted us . . . to think about the process of
thought and reason, and argument would follow. That summer, I learned much about myself. This teacher had me reflect
on knowledge and knowing, he had me questioning everything about myself, so that I could be built back up again, with
a clearer sense of my responsibilities to the written word, and
more familiarity with my own thinking about my own thinking. After [many] days exploring philosophy, we began to read
literature. Again, he wanted to know how we thought about
our thinking as we read literature from around the world. My
writing developed in concert with my thinking.

Connected Thinking

The quality of connected thinking is necessary for teachers to have in
their repertoire today. Defined as a fusion of interdisciplinary thinking and
an ability to forge links between curriculum content and student interests
and aptitudes, connected thinking can open doors for students to see the
relationships among history, language, art, architecture, math, and science.
At the same time, students can begin to see how their own abilities cross over
into all of those areas.

One of the students noted:

> My best teacher helped me explore all the intricate threads that tie back to language. Every day, I pored over grammar exercises and translations of passages. While the stories I translated at the time didn't particularly fascinate me, the words did. I felt like I was unlocking a secret code. I made connections to the architecture of other cultures, and began to see the classical forms everywhere I went. The language came alive for me in the connections, just as everything it connected to became more real as well. I now saw the world as a system.

Structures for Special Populations in Classrooms and Schools

Structures in the Classroom

Just as openness, use of metacognitive strategies, and connected thinking were common hallmarks of successful teachers in the case studies, a few common structures within the classroom were also identified as most helpful for these special population gifted students. These classroom features included organization, grouping, independent work/modules, and use of outside experts. Teachers need to plan for each of these features as a routine part of addressing the needs of these learners.

Classroom Organization for Success

Organizing classrooms for gifted learners with special needs requires teacher flexibility and advanced planning that go above and beyond the usual units of study. It requires teachers to plan a month in advance what students will study, what new topics learners with special needs might be interested in, and how to organize for successful work in the space available.

Teachers who work with these students may juggle multiple demands for their time and resources. Setting up workstations or centers in the classroom may be a good way to organize differentiated activities for some learners. Having tiered activities in centers and workstations that groups rotate through daily may provide the flexibility needed to serve these students in the ways suggested in this book.

In addition, collaboration with others in the school may help in the planning stages for effective lessons. For example, guidance counselors may be able to provide resources related to careers in the field of study. At the same time, the school librarian may help garner additional materials to be used in the classroom for targeted projects, saving students time in searching for resources and relevant readings.

Grouping

Research has long shown that ability grouping helps gifted students to achieve at higher levels (see Kulik & Kulik, 1984; Rogers, 2002, 2015). The same is true for gifted learners with special needs, who require the safety of working with students like themselves. A solid approach to grouping is one that takes into account student ability in specific domain tasks; educators should organize and reorganize groups based on assessment data in an ongoing way. Another important aspect of grouping is taking into consideration student interest, allowing students to work together with peers of similar domain aptitudes.

Independent Work/Modules

Students of advanced ability often need flexibility beyond what grouping with peers can provide. Many of them rate independent work at the highest level of benefit to their development, especially at the secondary level. This independent work can take many forms, from project-based work, to accelerated self-study, to open-ended exploration of topics of interest. Students can be given a menu of options to allow for choice in independent project work, or a template for organizing their study, or a contract that specifies outcomes and deadlines.

Use of Outside Experts

Classrooms can be enhanced by the use of outside speakers on topics being studied. Each month teachers could ask an expert to visit the classroom, sometimes to give a talk, sometimes to answer questions that have been planned in advance, and sometimes to converse with students about real-world issues and problems related to the topic at hand. Scientists from universities and labs are often available to provide such support, as are personnel from federal and state agencies. By bringing the outside world into the classroom, teachers can show students that their work is relevant in the real world. This technique also may offer a prelude to career exploration for some of these learners with special needs in the form of role models and/or future mentors.

Support Structures in Schools

In order for gifted learners with special needs to receive opportunities for intervention, support structures in schools must also be provided. The easiest way to accomplish this is by integrating the set of interventions needed into the way these structures function. The areas of greatest need for support are the ongoing professional development of teachers and principals; parent education; collaboration with universities and other outside agencies; flexible implementation of grouping, scheduling, and acceleration; and use of appropriate materials and assessments.

Professional Development

The professional development of teachers of the gifted and all classroom teachers is critical to successful teaching of gifted learners with special needs. Professional learning in this area helps educators to understand the characteristics and needs of these students, the techniques of creative and critical thinking, and how to apply the models to specific subject areas. Principals also need training in what to look for in the classroom when evaluating the effectiveness of teachers who work with gifted learners with special needs. Ongoing professional development for teachers who work directly with gifted learners is a critical component of ensuring that higher order skills and concepts are being taught well in gifted programs. Professional development should be focused on learning and applying selected critical thinking, creative problem solving, and concept development to advanced curriculum material in all subject domains. Teachers can become experts in a few models that they can apply to different content areas, or they can select materials where those applications have already been made (Dixon & Moon, 2015).

Parent Education

Parent education sessions are also important to hold across the course of a year. These sessions may focus on the following areas for dialogue and discussion:
- How to locate mentors or friends for your child
- How to select effective summer programs and camps
- How to incorporate the arts into your child's life
- The role of museums in family life
- The art of dinner table conversation
- Modeling creative habits of mind
- Modeling a love of knowledge

- Asking questions that promote critical thinking
- Discussing thought processes and how problems are solved as a family

If parents take an active role in promoting higher level thinking in their children at home, students perform better at school. A combined effort of school and home influences can only facilitate the future development of these gifted students with special needs toward greater creative productivity (Peterson, 2009; Peterson & Lorimer, 2011, 2012).

Collaboration With Universities and Agencies

Collaboration with universities may provide a source of mentors and tutors who have a special interest in working with special needs learners. Many minority students in college, for example, want to guide and help younger students who are traversing the path they walked years before as elementary and secondary students. College students from poverty may be excellent tutors for younger students who will likely be first generation college students (Ford, 2011, 2013). In addition, agencies such as science laboratories might provide resources for STEM development, which could help provide advanced opportunities in the math, science, and technology curriculum.

Flexible Implementation of Grouping, Scheduling, and Acceleration

Flexibility in grouping is central to ensuring that these students' needs are met. Many times the accommodations require individual changes to be made; other times changes need to be made for small groups. Sometimes time adjustments need to be made; content can either be shortened or lengthened to provide special opportunities. Scheduling of courses and classes also has to remain flexible to ensure that students have available opportunities that do not overlap with their schedules (Coleman & Johnsen, 2013).

An acceleration policy is a necessary component of a plan to serve learners with special needs. As demonstrated in the case studies, acceleration was the most important intervention the students engaged in during their years in school. Schools benefit from having an acceleration policy in place that addresses the need for early entrance and exit from various levels of schooling as well as advanced content opportunities at all stages of development (Assouline, Colangelo, & VanTassel-Baska, 2015; Assouline, Colangelo, VanTassel-Baska, & Lupkowski-Shoplik, 2015).

Use of Appropriate Materials and Assessments

Selection of materials that support differentiation is also a critical component of a successful program for these learners. It is unrealistic to expect that teachers will create material "on the fly" that will elevate the thinking skills of their students. The use of deliberate models embedded in research-based materials ensures that the appropriate skills are taught. Research-based exemplary materials have demonstrated effectiveness in teaching these skills in discrete subject areas and in more integrated programs (VanTassel-Baska, 2017).

Using appropriate assessment techniques is also an important and necessary component of developing the skills and concepts of gifted learners with special needs. If teachers do not assess higher level thinking and concept development, then students will not feel that they need to stretch themselves on various types of classroom assessments. Performance-based assessments that are open-ended yet require higher order thinking and creative problem solving are ideal for judging progress in this area of learning. Portfolio approaches that require students to select their best work from a particular learning period, reflect on their progress, and share their work with a real-world audience also provide important evidence of student growth in thinking and reasoning (VanTassel-Baska, 2008).

Parental Roles and Responsibilties

Parent involvement is central to any considerations for providing supportive services for special populations of learners (Niehaus & Adelson, 2014). The following suggestions are designed to help parents and teachers understand how best to work together with the school on students' behalf.

Advocacy at School

Parents need to consider themselves the primary advocates for their child. They often identify the complexities of the learning problems and abilities of their child before school personnel do. They see their child holistically, not as a set of labels or conditions. Parents of ELLs and learners from poverty will encounter more difficulty finding the resources needed to assist in their child's development. For these populations, more support in the form of translation services and special conferences may be required. A necessary part of these parents' advocacy role is establishing regular contact with their child's guidance counselor and teachers regarding opportunities and progress, using the parental liaison available in many schools. Parents should also have a critical role in the intervention implementation plan, especially if students do not have an IEP.

For teachers, parents can serve as a resource for providing missing data about a student's strengths and weaknesses. Many twice-exceptional students, for example, will display different behaviors at home than they do at school.

Thus, getting a 360-degree view of their behavior is helpful. Teachers may resent the involvement of parents, especially parents of twice-exceptional students who can recognize important behaviors in their child and feel that more should be done for them. Teachers, however, should view meetings with these parents as collaborative work sessions to provide students with interventions they need, rather than as combative interactions.

Monitoring Progress at Home

Parents routinely need access to their child's school assignments through electronic means or other forms of communication in order to keep up with student work. As articulated by Ralph's father (see p. 34), this system of communication was essential to understanding his son's progress in school and how he could help at home. Ralph's father felt strongly that his son would not have graduated without the school's individual class websites.

Parents need access to grades and other forms of teacher feedback so that they may assist in home follow-up on assignments not completed or turned in. This access gives parents insight into where communication problems might lie—with their child, with the school, with the teacher, or all three.

Supporting Learning at Home

Parents can provide students with home support in the form of books and other stimuli that feed their interests. At the primary level, puzzles and games may be used regularly. At intermediate levels, parents can stimulate interest in research by helping students begin collections of items of interest (e.g., postcards, bottle caps, etc.), categorizing them, and discussing their unique features. At secondary levels, parents can ensure that their child has access to films, lectures, groups, and discussions in areas that interest him or her and further educational goals in some way.

Because students from poverty may not have such support, teachers need to ensure that student requirements for projects do not involve a lot of home time and that resources are provided. Grading should be based on content and organization, not on physical presentation. Parents in these low-income households can provide support for the learning process through encouragement and acknowledging the importance of what the child is learning. All of these parents need access to information that can support the unique needs of their child.

Encouraging Interest in Education

Finally, parents are in a unique position to encourage their children to continue their education, to follow their interests and their passions. Although school may be frustrating for these learners, the home environment can be a safe haven where expectations focus on the learning process itself, not on its outcomes. Encourage parents to take walks in the woods with their child to examine leaves, help a child start collections of objects in nature, and discuss issues of the day at the dinner table. These can all be small ways to help focus these students on what they do well and what they enjoy doing in respect to learning. Playing games and doing puzzles together can alleviate the stress of facing the discrepancies of performance in school. Watching movies and television programs can be educational in respect to the ideas generated for meaningful discussions.

Implications for Gifted Education, ELL Programs, and Special Education

The implications for learners in respect to both identification and services provided are extensive for all professionals who work with these learners. The largest issue for personnel to consider is how to collaborate across programs that may operate as islands in a given school district. In areas such as identification and teacher training, the involvement of all relevant departments (i.e., gifted, special education, counseling, Title I, and ESOL) that govern the interventions for these students must be guaranteed.

Identification of special populations of learners must honor the need for flexibility in the processes employed so that students with free and reduced lunch, ELLs, and twice-exceptional students are not overlooked. The easiest way to ensure such consideration is to establish a fixed percentage of these students for inclusion in gifted programs. For example, a student who is twice-exceptional but not identified as gifted may perform at the B level in her classes, which could seem unremarkable to many. Teachers may not expect better performance from her, but she may need opportunities to engage with higher level material in order to show her full potential.

There is a misconception that students are overidentified for both gifted and special education services, yet evidence suggests that both exceptionalities are underidentified for service needs. Nationally, 12% of students are identified as gifted, with the same percentage for special education (NAGC, 2015). In many school districts the percentages are significantly higher, ranging upwards of 25% for gifted, based on the local population norms. Teachers should not be concerned about the absolute numbers identified; rather they should focus on the student intervention needs. Giftedness is a relative concept, after all, based on differences within the context of a given district population. In some settings, students who perform one standard deviation above the mean may be gifted. In other settings, the requirement would be two standard deviations above the mean. Decisions about who is identified for gifted programs and services should be based on local norms for the special needs groups—at least the top 10% of each group should be considered for gifted program services.

Beyond just identification, however, lie concerns about how best to service these students, given the difficulties in addressing sometimes conflicting profiles. Several students in this book's study presented as having contradictory needs, where weaknesses overwhelmed strengths at a point in their development or where the ability was masked by the disability. The following may help to clarify how this problem presents in these special needs learners.

Labeling. In the world of learners with special needs, where labeling precedes the possibility of service, labels become an important part of considering provisions. Yet, as demonstrated in several of the case studies, the number of labels needed to convey the range of problems these students face is too great to use that approach. Instead, clustering the problems faced so that interventions are integrative in nature can provide support in various areas in order to reach some of these students. Thus, it may be important to consider how to address through one intervention, rather than three different ones, a student's need for social awareness, for cognitive challenge, and metacognitive skill development. Although two out of the three may be considered deficits, using cognitive challenge to address both social and metacognitive weaknesses may be the right antidote to all three issues.

Conflicting intervention techniques. Another concern for programming for these students is how dual programs and services need to work together in order to be effective. For example, special education programs stress behavior modification in working with students who need regulation, such as students with ADHD or emotionally disturbed students, yet gifted education programs advocate more strongly for cognitive therapies as the best tools to reach these learners. Such differences may impact the counseling and guidance received, as well as the short-term classroom behavior approaches employed. Because service to the giftedness should lead interventions, educators must work together to ensure that gifted students with special needs are well-served.

Need for closer collaboration and support. Given the nature, severity, and extent of problems that these students face, educators must be especially diligent to ensure that close collaboration occurs in providing services and designing programs. To the extent possible, services should be integrated, not serialized in implementation. Although 504 plans and IEPs are good tools for specifying the simultaneous nature of the needed intervention, typically it is in the implementation of such plans where problems occur. Students may, for example, receive speech services while not receiving advanced English instruction where those skills could be practiced regularly.

Conclusion

The final section of this book has focused on support structures that are needed to ensure that gifted learners with special needs receive appropriate services in school communities. The stakeholders within every school community will have different backgrounds and different areas of expertise. Although educators may not automatically know who can help most effectively in a given area, they can still discuss individual student needs, using this book as a starting point. They also can still advocate for these students with the reproducible guide provided (see pp. 118–120). Teachers and their colleagues can learn still more from the resources in Parts II and III of this book, and other publications and web resources included in the Resources section.

Communication across disciplines and between different kinds of professionals within schools is necessary to promote greater understanding of student needs. Communication is the first step toward both advocacy and collaboration. Suggestions on ways to advocate and collaborate have been provided in this section, but these suggestions are by no means exhaustive. As long as educators are working with a common understanding about the nature and needs of these learners, collaboration can take many forms to benefit these students in their talent development process.

Support for these learners can come from many different sources, and it may come in many forms—from fiscal resources, to time for collaboration, to people who can provide mentorships or tailor programs that are well-organized and focus on results. Agencies and schools must work together on behalf of these students to optimize their education.

Final Thoughts

This text has provided an overview of past and present research on the nature and needs of gifted English language learners, gifted students of poverty, and twice-exceptional learners. The authors included their own research in the form of qualitative case studies. Through the lives of 10 students, this book has examined their reflections on the learning process, and discussed what worked best for them in their educational journey. The 10 young people profiled in the text represent a collection of conditions that often disadvantage learners for achievement and success in school and beyond.

For many special populations of gifted learners, a high school diploma is farther out of reach than for their general education peers. According to the NCES, in 2013–2014 the graduation rate for economically disadvantaged students was 75%. For ELLs, the average was 63%. Students with learning disabilities also had a graduation rate of 63%. All three groups had a lower graduation rate than the overall national average of 82% (NCES, 2016). In addition, graduation rates from college for low-income students who are gifted are also lower than for more advantaged students (Wyner et al., 2007).

Many of the students in this book's study faced multiple factors related to specific learning disabilities, other health impairments, poverty, second language status, or all of the above. All of these students needed the interventions they received to actualize their potential, giving them the capacity to overcome adversity in school and graduate on time or even early.

All of the students went beyond the standard diploma requirements measured by the National Center for Educational Statistics. All of these students received an advanced diploma from high school, indicating higher levels of coursework, particularly in math and foreign language. Almost all of the students went on to a 4-year university, and some of them have already graduated from college. The giftedness that each possesses has allowed him or her to rise above conditions of poverty, disability, and second language acquisition.

Although not all of the students felt equally successful in high school, college, or their current trajectories, they all did experience success in at least one area of their scholastic careers. They all experienced interventions that helped them in their talent development. Their stories compel educators to reconsider the nature and scope of interventions they provide for such students in schools.

Part II of the book outlined the nature of interventions that proved successful for these learners, often in their own words. Teachers can read and use the lesson plans presented as a model for how they might implement a particular approach or curricular innovation. These interventions provide a sense of the diversity of approaches that work for these learners, from cognitive, to affective, to aesthetic approaches. They also highlight the role of open-ended inquiry in the form of questions and activities on which these students thrive.

Part III of the book provided important ideas for support structures needed for effective implementation of the interventions listed. If teachers and administrators are unwilling or unable to support the flexibility necessary to respond to the needs of these dually labeled learners, then the intervention plans will not succeed. When school personnel are prepared to be flexible, the chances of success rise significantly. The book concluded with caveats around the continuing problems and issues these students will encounter on their educational journeys, even when provisions have been made for them.

In the end, however, it is the people who step forward to help who are the most significant in the lives of gifted students with special needs. Those who nurture these students and their talents are the heroes of these stories, too.

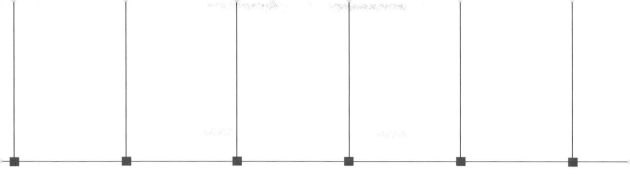

Resources

The following resources have been selected to assist teachers in assessing and teaching gifted learners with special needs in their strength areas. The authors hope that these resources will also be shared among teachers to ensure a diffusion of helpful information on this topic.

Print Resources

Adelson, J., Carroll, S., Casa, T., Gavin, K., Sheffield, L., & Spinelli, A. (2007). Project M3: Mentoring mathematical minds: A research-based curriculum for talented elementary students. *Journal of Advanced Academics*, 18(4), 26–37.

Assouline, S., Colangelo, N., & VanTassel-Baska, J. (2015). *A nation empowered: Evidence trumps the excuses that hold back America's brightest students* (Vol. 1). Iowa City: University of Iowa, The Connie Belin & Jacqueline N. Blank International Center for Gifted Education and Talent Development.

Assouline, S., Colangelo, N., VanTassel-Baska, J., & Lupkowski-Shoplik, A. (Eds.). (2015). *A nation empowered: Evidence trumps the excuses that hold back America's brightest students* (Vol. 2). Iowa City: University of Iowa, The Connie Belin & Jacqueline N. Blank International Center for Gifted Education and Talent Development.

Baska, A., & VanTassel-Baska, J. (2014). *Ancient roots and ruins: A guide to understanding the Romans, their world, and their language.* Waco, TX: Prufrock Press.

Colangelo, N., Assouline, S. G., & Gross, M. U. M. (2004). *A nation deceived: How schools hold back America's brightest students* (Vol. 1). Iowa City: The University of Iowa, The Connie Belin & Jacqueline N. Blank International Center for Gifted Education and Talent Development.

Colangelo, N., Assouline, S. G., & Gross, M. U. M. (Eds.). (2004). *A nation deceived: How schools hold back America's brightest students* (Vol. 2). Iowa City: The University of Iowa, The Connie Belin & Jacqueline N. Blank International Center for Gifted Education and Talent Development.

Department of Education, Office of English Language Acquisition. (2015). *Tools and resources for providing English learners equal access to curricular and extracurricular programs.* Retrieved from https://www2.ed.gov/about/offices/list/oela/english-learner-toolkit/chap4.pdf

Dixon, F., & Moon, S. (2015). *The handbook of secondary gifted education* (2nd ed.). Waco, TX: Prufrock Press.

Ford, D. Y. (2011). *Reversing underachievement among gifted black students* (2nd ed.). Waco, TX: Prufrock Press.

Halsted, J. W. (2009). *Some of my best friends are books: Guiding gifted readers* (3rd ed.). Scottsdale, AZ: Great Potential Press.

Johnsen, S. (Ed.). (2012). *NAGC Pre-K–Grade 12 Gifted Education Programming Standards: A guide to planning and implementing high-quality services.* Waco, TX: Prufrock Press.

Lewis, L. C., Rivera, A., & Roby, D. (2012). *Identifying and serving culturally and linguistically diverse gifted students.* Waco, TX: Prufrock Press.

Matthews, M. A., & Castellano, J. A. (Eds.). (2014). *Talent development for English language learners: Identifying and developing potential.* Waco, TX: Prufrock Press.

Neihart, M., & Poon, K. (2009). *Gifted children with autism spectrum disorders.* Waco, TX: Prufrock Press.

Siegle, D. (2013). *The underachieving gifted child: Recognizing, understanding, and reversing underachievement.* Waco, TX: Prufrock Press.

Stambaugh, T., & VanTassel-Baska, J. (2016). *Jacob's Ladder Reading Comprehension Program: Nonfiction, grade 3.* Waco, TX: Prufrock Press.

Stambaugh, T., & VanTassel-Baska, J. (2017). *Jacob's Ladder Reading Comprehension Program: Grades 6–7* (2nd ed.). Waco, TX: Prufrock Press.

Stambaugh, T., & Wood, S. M. (2015). *Serving gifted students in rural settings.* Waco, TX: Prufrock Press.

VanTassel-Baska, J. (Ed.). (2008). *Alternative assessments with gifted and talented students.* Waco, TX: Prufrock Press.

VanTassel-Baska, J., & Avery, L. (2012). *Changing tomorrow 1: A leadership unit for elementary students.* Waco, TX: Prufrock Press.

VanTassel-Baska, J., & Stambaugh, T. (2016). *Jacob's Ladder Reading Comprehension Program: Nonfiction, grade 4.* Waco, TX: Prufrock Press.

Van Tassel-Baska, J., & Stambaugh, T. (2016). *Jacob's Ladder Reading Comprehension Program: Nonfiction, grade 5*. Waco, TX: Prufrock Press.

Van Tassel-Baska, J., & Stambaugh, T. (2017). *Jacob's Ladder Reading Comprehension Program: Grades 7–8* (2nd ed.). Waco, TX: Prufrock Press.

Van Tassel-Baska, J., & Stambaugh, T. (Eds.). (2018). Special issue: Gifted students from low-income households. *Gifted Child Quarterly, 62,* 1–144.

Van Tassel-Baska, J. L., Cross, T. L., & Olenchak, F. R. (2009). *Social-emotional curriculum with gifted and talented students*. Waco, TX: Prufrock Press.

Weinfeld, R., Barnes-Robinson, L., Jeweler, S., & Shevitz, B. R. (2013). *Smart kids with learning difficulties: Overcoming obstacles and realizing potential* (2nd ed.). Waco, TX: Prufrock Press.

Web-Based Resources

The following websites and webpages are included to aid educators in the process of advocating and providing services for gifted learners with special needs.

A Nation Deceived
https://www.accelerationinstitute.org/Nation_Deceived/Get_Report.aspx

This webpage provides access to a policy report on acceleration practices in schools.

Tips for Teachers Video Series from Children and Adults with Attention-Deficit/Hyperactivity Disorder (CHADD)
http://www.chadd.org/Understanding-ADHD/For-Professionals/For-Teachers/Tips-for-Teachers-Video-Series.aspx

CHADD focuses on providing resources for ADHD disorders to parents and professionals. This specific video series is designed to help teachers plan effectively for such students in the classroom.

Council for Exceptional Children
https://www.cec.sped.org

This national organization focuses on students with special needs, including gifted and exceptional populations. The CEC website provides resources, such as publications and website media.

Hoagies' Gifted Education Page

http://www.hoagiesgifted.org

Designed for teachers and parents of the gifted, this website includes resources on a variety of topics in gifted education.

International Children's Digital Library

http://en.childrenslibrary.org

This website is devoted to providing children's literature online in many different languages with available translations to English.

National Association for Gifted Children

https://nagc.org

This national organization is devoted to the needs of the gifted and provides access to many free resources.

National Clearinghouse for English Language Acquisition

https://ncela.ed.gov

This website is devoted to providing quality resources for teachers and others on English language learners.

References

Adams, C. M., & Chandler, K. L. (2014). *Effective program models for gifted students from underserved populations.* Waco, TX: Prufrock Press.

Adler, M. J. (1984). *The Paideia program: An educational syllabus.* Chicago, IL: Institute for Philosophical Research.

Aguirre, N. M., & Hernandez, N. E. (2011). Differentiating the curriculum for gifted second language learners: Teaching them to think. In J. A. Castellano & A. D. Frazier (Eds.), *Special populations in gifted education: Understanding our most able students from diverse backgrounds* (pp. 273–286). Waco, TX: Prufrock Press.

Ambrose, D. (2013). Socioeconomic inequality and giftedness: Suppression and distortion of high ability. *Roeper Review, 35,* 81–92.

American Community Survey. (2015). *Census Bureau reports at least 350 languages spoken in U.S. homes* (Release No. CB15-185). Washington, DC: Author.

American Psychiatric Association. (1987). *Diagnostic and statistical manual of mental disorders* (3rd ed., Revised). Washington, DC: Author.

American Psychiatric Association. (1994). *Diagnostic and statistical manual of mental disorders* (4th ed.). Washington, DC: Author.

American Psychiatric Association. (2013). *Diagnostic and statistical manual of mental disorders* (5th ed.). Washington, DC: Author.

Angelelli, C., Enright, K., & Valdés, G. (2002). *Developing the talents and abilities of linguistically gifted bilingual students: Guidelines for developing curriculum at the high school level.* Storrs: University of Connecticut, National Research Center on Gifted Education.

Arias, M. B., & Morillo-Campbell, M. (2008). *Promoting ELL parental involvement: Challenges in contested times.* East Lansing, MI: The Great Lakes Center for Education Research & Practice.

Assouline, S., Colangelo, N., & VanTassel-Baska, J. (2015). *A nation empowered: Evidence trumps the excuses that hold back America's brightest students* (Vol. 1). Iowa City: University of Iowa, The Connie Belin & Jacqueline N. Blank International Center for Gifted Education and Talent Development.

Assouline, S., Colangelo, N., VanTassel-Baska, J., & Lupkowski-Shoplik, A. (Eds.). (2015). *A nation empowered: Evidence trumps the excuses that hold back America's brightest students* (Vol. 2). Iowa City: University of Iowa, The Connie Belin & Jacqueline N. Blank International Center for Gifted Education and Talent Development.

Baska, A., & VanTassel-Baska, J. (2014). *Ancient roots and ruins: A guide to understanding the Romans, their world, and their language.* Waco, TX: Prufrock Press.

Baska, A., & VanTassel-Baska, J. (2016). Portraits of high potential-high need students: The role of teacher inquiry. *LEARNing Landscapes, 9*(2), 69–85.

Baum, S. M., Cooper, C. R., & Neu, T. W. (2001). Dual differentiation: An approach to meeting the curricular needs of gifted students with learning disabilities. *Psychology in the Schools, 38,* 477–490.

Baum, S., Owens, S. V., & Dixon, J. (2017). *To be gifted and learning disabled: Strength-based strategies for helping twice-exceptional students with LD, ADHD, ASD, and more* (3rd ed.). Waco, TX: Prufrock Press.

Beck, I., & McKeown, M. (2007). Increasing young low-income children's oral vocabulary repertoires through rich and focused instruction. *The Elementary School Journal, 107,* 251–271.

Benbow, C. P. (1991). Meeting the needs of gifted students through the use of acceleration. In M. C. Wang, M. C. Reynolds, & H. J. Walberg (Eds.), *Handbook of special education* (Vol. 4, pp. 23–36). Elmsford, NY: Pergamon.

Berninger, V., & Abbott, R. (2013). Differences between children with dyslexia who are and are not gifted in verbal reasoning. *Gifted Child Quarterly, 57,* 223–233.

Bianco, M., & Harris, B. (2014). Strength-based RTI: Developing gifted potential in Spanish-speaking English language learners. *Gifted Child Today, 37,* 169–176.

Briggs, C., Reis, S. M., & Sullivan, E. (2008). A national view of promising programs and practices for culturally, linguistically, and ethnically diverse gifted and talented students. *Gifted Child Quarterly, 52,* 131–145.

Brody, L. (2004). *Grouping and acceleration practices in gifted education.* Thousand Oaks, CA: Corwin Press.

Burney, V. H., & Beilke, J. R. (2008). The constraints of poverty on high achievement. *Journal of the Education of the Gifted, 31,* 171–197.

Center for Gifted Education, William & Mary. (n.d.). *Literature web.* Retrieved from https://education.wm.edu/centers/cfge/_documents/curriculum/teachingmodels/literatureweb.pdf

Chetty, R., Hendren, N., Kline, P., Saez, E., & Turner, N. (2014). Is the United States still a land of opportunity? Recent trends in intergenerational mobility. *The American Economic Review, 104*(5), 141–147.

Colangelo, N., Assouline, S. G., & Gross, M. U. M. (2004a). *A nation deceived: How schools hold back America's brightest students* (Vol. 1). Iowa City: The University of Iowa, The Connie Belin & Jacqueline N. Blank International Center for Gifted Education and Talent Development.

Colangelo, N., Assouline, S. G., & Gross, M. U. M. (Eds.). (2004b). *A nation deceived: How schools hold back America's brightest students* (Vol. 2). Iowa City: The University of Iowa, The Connie Belin & Jacqueline N. Blank International Center for Gifted Education and Talent Development.

Coleman, M. R., & Johnsen, S. K. (2013). *Implementing RtI with gifted students: Service models, trends, and issues.* Waco, TX: Prufrock Press.

Creswell, J. W., & Creswell, J. B. (2018). *Research design: Qualitative, quantitative, and mixed methods approaches* (5th ed.). Thousand Oaks, CA: SAGE.

Daurio, S. P. (1979). Educational enrichment versus acceleration: A review of the literature. In W. C. George, S. J. Cohn, & J. C. Stanley (Eds.), *Educating the gifted: Acceleration and enrichment* (pp. 13–53). Baltimore, MD: Johns Hopkins University Press.

Dixon, F. A., & Moon, S. M. (2015). *The handbook of secondary gifted education* (2nd ed.). Waco, TX: Prufrock Press.

Dulong-Langley, S. (2017). Curricular considerations for advanced English language learners. In J. VanTassel-Baska & C. A. Little (Eds.), *Content-based curriculum for high-ability learners* (3rd ed., pp. 63–78). Waco, TX: Prufrock Press.

Farkas, S., Duffett, A., & Loveless, T. (2008) *High-achieving students in an era of No Child Left Behind.* Washington DC: Fordham Institute.

Fecho, B. (2004). *Is this English? Race, language, and culture in the classroom.* New York, NY: Teachers College Press.

Foley Nicpon, M., Allmon, A., Sieck, B., & Stinson, R. D. (2011). Empirical investigation of twice-exceptionality: Where have we been and where are we going? *Gifted Child Quarterly, 55,* 3–17.

Foley Nicpon, M., Assouline, S. G., Schuler, P., & Amend, E. R. (2010). Gifted and talented students on the autism spectrum: Best practices for fostering talent and accommodating concerns. In J. A. Castellano & A. D. Frazier, (Eds.) *Special populations in gifted education: Understanding our most able students from diverse backgrounds* (pp. 227–248). Waco, TX: Prufrock Press.

Ford, D. Y. (2011). *Reversing underachievement among gifted black students* (2nd ed.). Waco, TX: Prufrock Press.

Ford, D. Y. (2013). *Recruiting and retaining culturally different students in gifted education.* Waco, TX: Prufrock Press.

Ford, D. Y., & Kea, C. D. (2009). Creating culturally responsive instruction: For students' sake and teachers' sake. *Focus on Exceptional Children, 41*(9), 1–18.

Frank, A. J., & McBee, M. T. (2003). The use of *Harry Potter and the Sorcerer's Stone* to discuss identity development with gifted adolescents. *Journal of Secondary Gifted Education, 15,* 33–41.

Gallagher, S., & Gallagher, J. J. (2002). Giftedness and Asperger's syndrome: A new agenda for education. *Understanding Our Gifted, 14*(2), 1–9.

Gallagher, S., & Stepien, W. (1996). Content acquisition in problem-based learning: Depth versus breadth in American studies. *Journal for the Education of the Gifted, 19,* 257–275.

Gavin, M. K., Casa, T., Adelson, J. L., Carroll, S. R., & Sheffield, L. J. (2009). The impact of advanced curriculum on the achievement of mathematically promising elementary students. *Gifted Child Quarterly, 53,* 188–202.

Goldenberg, C. (2008). Teaching English language learners: What the research does—and does not—say. *American Educator, 32*(2), 8–23, 42–44.

Gross, M. U. M. (2004). *Exceptionally gifted children* (2nd ed.). Sydney, Australia: Routledge.

Halsted, J. W. (2009). *Some of my best friends are books: Guiding gifted readers* (3rd ed.). Scottsdale, AZ: Great Potential Press.

Hodgkinson, H. (2007). Leaving too many children behind: A demographer's view on the neglect of America's youngest children. In J. VanTassel-Baska & T. Stambaugh (Eds.) *Overlooked gems: A national perspective on low-income promising learners* (pp. 7–20). Washington, DC: National Association for Gifted Children.

Howley, C., Howley, A., & Showalter, D. (2015). Leaving or staying home: Belief systems and paradigms. In T. Stambaugh & S. Wood (Eds.) *Serving gifted students in rural settings* (pp. 23–51). Waco, TX: Prufrock Press.

Hughes, C. E. (2011). Twice-exceptional learners: Twice the challenges, twice the joys. In J. Castellano & A. D. Frazier (Eds.), *Special populations in gifted education: Understanding our most able students from diverse backgrounds* (pp. 153–174). Waco, TX: Prufrock Press.

Hughes, C. E., Kettler, T., Shaunessey-Dedrick, E., & VanTassel-Baska, J. (2014). *A teacher's guide to using the Common Core State Standards with gifted and advanced learners in the English language arts.* Waco, TX: Prufrock Press.

Jiang, Y., Ekono, M., & Skinner, C. (2016). *Basic facts about low-income children: Children under 18 years, 2014.* New York, NY: National Center on Children in Poverty. Retrieved from http://www.nccp.org/publications/pub_1145.html

Johnsen, S. (Ed.). (2012). *NAGC Pre-K–Grade 12 Gifted Education Programming Standards: A guide to planning and implementing high-quality services.* Waco, TX: Prufrock Press.

Kennedy, D. M., Banks, R. S., & Grandin, T. (2011). *Bright not broken: Gifted kids, ADHD, and autism.* San Francisco, CA: Jossey-Bass.

Kirk, S., Gallagher, J., & Coleman, M. R. (2014). *Educating exceptional children.* Stamford, CT: Cengage Learning.

Kulik, J. A., & Kulik, C. C. (1984). Effects of accelerated instruction on students. *Review of Educational Research, 54,* 409–425.

Lakin, J. M., & Lohman, D. F. (2011). The predictive accuracy of verbal, quantitative, and nonverbal reasoning tests: Consequences for talent identification and program diversity. *Journal for the Education of the Gifted, 34,* 595–623.

Lee, O., & Buxton, C. A. (2013). Teacher professional development to improve science and literacy achievement of English language learners. *Theory Into Practice, 52,* 110–117.

Lyman, R., Sanders, E., Abbott, R., & Berninger, V. (2017). Translating interdisciplinary research on language learning into identifying specific learning disabilities in verbally gifted and average children and youth. *Journal of Behavioral and Brain Research, 7*(6).

McClain, M.-C., & Pfeiffer, S. (2012). Identification of gifted students in the United States today: A look at state definitions, policies, and practices. *Journal of Applied School Psychology, 28,* 59–88.

McClarty, K. L. (2015). Life in the fast lane: Effects of early grade acceleration on high school and college outcomes. *Gifted Child Quarterly, 59*(1), 3–13.

McDonald, D., & Farrell, T. (2012). Out of the mouths of babes: Early college high school students' transformational learning experiences. *Journal of Advanced Academics, 23,* 217–248.

Miller, A. (2002). *Mentoring students and young people: A handbook of effective practice.* London, England: Routledge.

National Association for Gifted Children. (2011). *Identifying and serving culturally and linguistically diverse gifted students* [Position Statement]. Washington, DC: Author.

National Association for Gifted Children. (2015). *State of the states report.* Washington, DC: Author.

National Center for Education Statistics. (2015). *Fast facts: English language learners.* Retrieved from http://nces.ed.gov/fastfacts/display.asp?id=96

National Center for Education Statistics. (2016). *Common Core of Data: Public high school 4-year adjusted cohort graduation rate (ACGR), by race/ethnicity and selected demographics for the United States, the 50 states, and the District of Columbia: School year 2014–15.* Retrieved from https://nces.ed.gov/ccd/tables/ACGR_RE_and_characteristics_2014-15.asp

Neihart, M. (2008). Identifying and providing services to twice-exceptional children. In S. I. Pfeiffer (Ed.), *Handbook of giftedness in children* (pp. 115–137). New York, NY: Springer.

Neihart, M., & Poon, K. (2009). *Gifted children with autism spectrum disorders.* Waco, TX: Prufrock Press.

Niehaus, K., & Adelson, J. L. (2014). School support, parental involvement, and academic and social-emotional outcomes for English language learners. *American Educational Research Journal, 4,* 810–844.

Olszewski-Kubilius, P., & Clarenbach, J. (2014). Closing the opportunity gap: Program factors contributing to academic success in culturally different youth. *Gifted Child Today, 37,* 103–110.

Olszewski-Kubilius, P., Steenbergen-Hu, S., Thomsen, D., & Rosen, R. (2017). Minority achievement gaps in STEM: Findings of a longitudinal study of Project Excite. *Gifted Child Quarterly, 61,* 20–39.

Park, G., Lubinski, D., & Benbow, C. P. (2013). When less is more: Effects of grade skipping on adult STEM productivity among mathematically precocious adolescents. *Journal of Educational Psychology, 105,* 176–198.

Peterson, J. S. (2009). Focusing on where they are: A clinical perspective. In J. L. VanTassel-Baska, T. L. Cross, & F. R. Olenchak (Eds.), *Social-emotional curriculum with gifted and talented students* (pp. 193–226). Waco, TX: Prufrock Press.

Peterson, J., & Lorimer, M. (2011). Student response to a small-group affective curriculum in a school for gifted children. *Gifted Child Quarterly, 55,* 167–180.

Peterson, J., & Lorimer, M. (2012). Small-group affective curriculum for gifted students: A longitudinal study of teacher-facilitators. *Roeper Review, 34,* 158–169.

Plucker, J. A., Hardesty, J., & Burroughs, N. (2013). *Talent on the sidelines: Excellence gaps and America's persistent talent underclass.* Storrs: Center for Education Policy Analysis, University of Connecticut.

Reis, S. M., McCoach, D. B., Little, C. A., Muller, L. M., & Kaniskan, R. B. (2011). The effects of differentiated instruction and enrichment pedagogy on reading achievement in five elementary schools. *American Educational Research Journal, 48,* 462–501.

Reynolds, M., Birch, J., & Tuseth, A. (1962). Review of research on early admission. In M. Reynolds (Ed.), *Early school admission for mentally advanced children* (pp. 7–18). Reston, VA: Council for Exceptional Children.

Rogers, K. B. (2002). *Re-forming gifted education.* Scottsdale, AZ: Great Potential Press.

Rogers, K. B. (2015). The academic, socialization, and psychological effects of acceleration: Research synthesis. In S. G. Assouline, N. Colangelo, J. VanTassel-Baska, & A. Lupkowski-Shoplik (Eds.), *A nation empowered: Evidence trumps the excuses that hold back America's brightest students* (Vol. 2, pp. 19–30). Iowa City: University of Iowa, The Connie Belin & Jacqueline N. Blank International Center for Gifted Education and Talent Development.

Siegle, D. (2013). *The underachieving gifted child: Recognizing, understanding, and reversing underachievement.* Waco, TX: Prufrock Press.

Siegle, D., & McCoach, D. B. (2005). Motivating gifted students. In F. A. Karnes & K. R. Stephens (Series Eds.), *The practical strategies series in gifted education.* Waco, TX: Prufrock Press.

Stambaugh, T., & Chandler, K. (2012). *Effective curriculum for underserved gifted students.* Waco, TX: Prufrock Press.

Stambaugh, T., & Wood, S. M. (Eds.). (2015). *Serving gifted students in rural settings.* Waco, TX: Prufrock Press.

Steenbergen-Hu, C., Makel, M., & Olszewski-Kubilius, P. (2016). What 100 years of research says about the effects of ability grouping and acceleration on K–12 students' academic achievement. *Review of Educational Research, 86,* 849–899.

Subotnik, R. F., & Steiner, C. L. (1994). Adult manifestations of adolescent talent in science: A longitudinal study of 1983 Westinghouse science talent search winners. In R. F. Subotnik & K. D. Arnold (Eds.), *Beyond Terman: Contemporary longitudinal studies of giftedness and talent* (pp. 52–76). Norwood, NJ: Ablex.

Sullivan, A. K., & Strang, H. R. (2002). Bibliotherapy in the classroom: Using literature to promote the development of emotional intelligence. *Childhood Education, 79,* 74–81.

Swiatek, M., & Benbow, C. (1991). Ten-year longitudinal follow-up of ability-matched accelerated and unaccelerated gifted students. *Journal of Educational Psychology, 83,* 528–538.

Trail, B. A. (2011). *Twice-exceptional gifted children: Understanding, teaching, and counseling gifted students.* Waco, TX: Prufrock Press.

Treffinger, D., Isaksen, S. G., & Dorval, K. B. (2006). *Creative problem solving: An introduction* (4th ed.). Waco, TX: Prufrock Press.

VanTassel-Baska, J. (Ed.). (2008). *Alternative assessments with gifted and talented students.* Waco, TX: Prufrock Press.

VanTassel-Baska, J. (Ed.). (2010). *Patterns and profiles of promising learners from poverty.* Waco, TX: Prufrock Press.

VanTassel-Baska, J. (2017). Achievement unlocked: Effective curriculum interventions with low-income students. *Gifted Child Quarterly, 62,* 68–82.

Vantassel-Baska, J., Buckingham, B. L. E., & Baska, A. (2009). The role of the arts in the socioemotional development of the gifted. In J. VanTassel-Baska, T. L. Cross, & F.R. Olenchak (Eds.), *Social-emotional curriculum with gifted and talented students* (pp. 227–258). Waco, TX: Prufrock Press

VanTassel-Baska, J., Feng, A. X., & de Brux, E. (2007). A study of identification and achievement profiles of performance task-identified gifted students over 6 years. *Journal for the Education of the Gifted, 31,* 7–34.

VanTassel-Baska, J., Johnson, D., & Avery, L. D. (2002). Using performance tasks in the identification of economically disadvantaged and minority gifted learners: Findings from Project STAR. *Gifted Child Quarterly, 46,* 110–123.

VanTassel-Baska, J., & Little, C. A. (Eds.). (2017). *Content-based curriculum for high-ability learners* (3rd ed.). Waco, TX: Prufrock Press.

VanTassel-Baska, J., MacFarlane, B., & Baska, A. (2017). *Second language learning for the gifted.* Washington, DC: National Association for Gifted Children.

VanTassel-Baska, J., McIntosh, J. S., & Kearney, K. L. (2015). Secondary affective curriculum and instruction for gifted learners. In F. A. Dixon & S. M. Moon (Eds.), *The handbook of secondary education* (2nd ed., pp. 509–540). Waco, TX: Prufrock Press.

VanTassel-Baska, J., & Stambaugh, T. (2006). Project Athena: A pathway to advanced literacy development for children of poverty. *Gifted Child Today, 29,* 58–65.

VanTassel-Baska, J., & Stambaugh, T. (2007). *Overlooked gems: A national perspective on low-income promising learners.* Washington, DC: National Association for Gifted Children.

VanTassel-Baska, J., & Stambaugh, T. (2018). *Affective Jacob's Ladder Reading Comprehension Program (Grades 4–5).* Waco, TX: Prufrock Press.

VanTassel-Baska, J., & Subotnik, R. (2004). *Background variables of participants in two contrasting models of highly selective out of school science programs: A preliminary analysis.* Presentation at the 51st Annual Convention of the National Association for Gifted Children, Salt Lake City, Utah, USA.

Weinfeld, R., Barnes-Robinson, L., Jeweler, S., & Shevitz, B. R. (2013). *Smart kids with learning difficulties: Overcoming obstacles and realizing potential.* Waco, TX: Prufrock Press.

Wood, S. M., & Lane, E. M. (2017). Using the Integrated Curriculum Model to address social, emotional, and career needs of advanced learners. In J. VanTassel-Baska & C. A. Little (Eds.), *Content-based curriculum for high-ability learners* (3rd ed., pp. 523–541). Waco, TX: Prufrock Press.

Worrell, F. C. (2014). Ethnically diverse students. In J. A. Plucker & C. M. Callahan (Eds.), *Critical issues and practices in gifted education: What the research says* (2nd ed., pp. 237–255). Waco, TX: Prufrock Press.

Wyner, J. S., Bridgeland, J. M., & DiIulio, J. J. (2007). *Achievement trap: How America is failing millions of high-achieving students from low-income families.* Washington, DC: Jack Kent Cooke Foundation.

Appendix A:
Literature Web

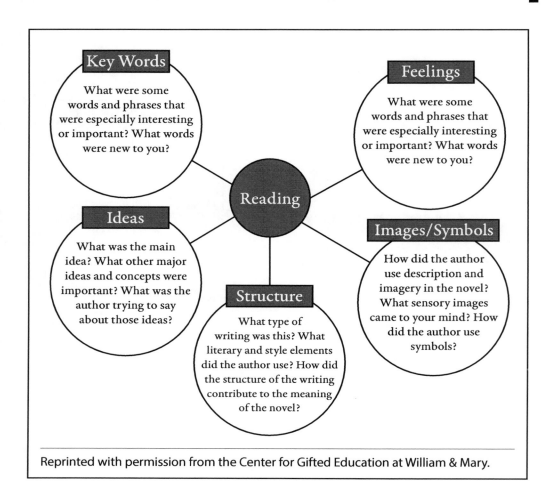

Reprinted with permission from the Center for Gifted Education at William & Mary.

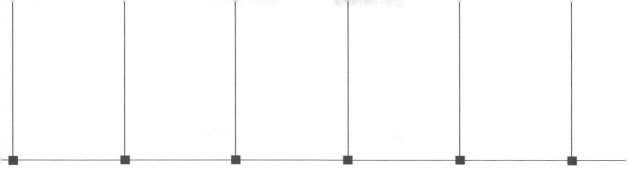

Appendix B:
Independent
Learning Contract

Independent Study Contract—First Quarter

1. Student Name: _____

2. Date: _____

3. Topic or Unit to Be Covered:

    _____

    _____

4. Resources to Be Used:

    _____

    _____

5. Unit Assessment:

    _____

    _____

6. Due Date: _____

7. Weekly goal-setting: Once per week, _____ and I will discuss

    goals for the upcoming week, in respect to _____

    _____ (specify skills).

8. Self-assessments (reflections on classwork and homework) are due at the end of every day of class.

9. Student Signature: _____

10. Parent Signature:_____

Appendix C: Quarterly Survey With Responses

The following is an example of a student survey distributed to a Latin class. Teachers can use this example to create their own surveys to learn what approaches worked with their students, as well as their students' level of engagement with the course material. These results, then, may be used for planning and structuring group opportunities for students.

Latin 2–Second Quarter Survey

1. How much effort do you think you put into school last quarter? (circle one)

   Very little effort   Lots of effort

   1   **2**   **3**   **4**   **5**

   Average 3.8

2. How much effort do you think you put into Latin last quarter? (circle one)

   Very little effort   Lots of effort

   1   **2**   **3**   **4**   **5**

   Average 3.3

3. How often do you study your Latin grammar/vocabulary? (circle one)

   Never   Quite often

   1   **2**   **3**   **4**   **5**

   Average 2.5

4. What do you think of the pace of this class?

Much too slow	Somewhat slow	About right	Somewhat fast	Much too fast
4 students	*6 students*	*18 students*	*4 students*	*8 students*

5. If you could change anything about this class, what would you change?
   - Less homework; 6/40 students
   - Weekly quizzes; 5/40 students
   - Fewer projects; 2/40 students
   - Go slower
   - More group work
   - More structure
   - More derivative lists
   - Move around more
   - How we learn vocab
   - Grading system

- Make vocab flashcards optional
- More information on writing in Latin
- Homework too repetitive
- More review
- More videos

6. What is one class activity (e.g., Vocab Flashcards, Quizlet Live, etc.—not videos or projects) from the last quarter that you would like to see again?
   - Quizlet Live; 12/54 students
   - Vocab Flashcards; 8/54 students
   - Aeneas on the Deck
   - Classroom Latin/Conversation

7. What are two things you want to study more in Latin?
   - Roman constitution
   - Conversational Latin
   - Imperial era
   - Mythology; 10 students
   - History; 5 students
   - Dress
   - Colors
   - Animals
   - Derivatives
   - Food
   - Alphabet/pronunciation
   - Indirect object
   - Modern songs in Latin
   - Write our own quizzes

8. Please list up to three things that you've identified that specifically help you to learn material better or more quickly (e.g., flashcards, singing, repetition, discussion, etc.).
   - Picture flashcards
   - Online quizzes
   - Bingo
   - Roots
   - Quizzing each other
   - Vocab squares

- Repetition
- Discussion
- Acting out
- Rhyming
- Singing
- Derivatives
- Funny things to "make it stick"
- Worksheets
- Flipbooks

About the Authors

Ariel Baska teaches all levels of Latin in Fairfax County Public Schools. She received her bachelor's degree in Classics from the College of William & Mary. She received her master's degree in curriculum studies with an emphasis in gifted education at George Mason University. She was the 2015 recipient of the A. Harry Passow Award from the National Association for Gifted Children (NAGC), in recognition of her work with gifted students in the classroom. She has written several articles and book chapters on different topics in gifted education and has presented at many national and international conferences on the topics of gifted education, foreign language education, and the classics. In collaboration with Joyce VanTassel-Baska, she cowrote a Latin curriculum guide for elementary and middle school gifted students, *Ancient Roots and Ruins* (2013). She also coauthored the book *Second Language Learning for the Gifted* (2017), part of the NAGC Select series.

Joyce VanTassel-Baska, Ed.D., is the Jody and Layton Smith Professor Emerita of Education and former Executive Director of the Center for Gifted Education at William & Mary in Virginia, where she developed a graduate program and a research and development center in gifted education. She also initiated and directed the Center for Talent Development at Northwestern University. Prior to her work in higher education, Dr. VanTassel-Baska served as the state director of gifted programs for Illinois, as a regional director of a gifted service center in the Chicago area, as coordinator of gifted programs for the Toledo, OH, public school system, and as a teacher of gifted high school students in English and Latin. She is past president of The Association for the Gifted of the Council for Exceptional Children, the Northwestern University Chapter of Phi Delta Kappa, and the National Association for Gifted Children.

Dr. VanTassel-Baska has published widely, including 30 books and more than 650 refereed journal articles, book chapters, and scholarly reports. Recent books include: *Content-Based Curriculum for High-Ability Learners* (3rd ed., 2017, with Catherine Little) and the *Jacob's Ladder Reading Comprehension Program* (2016–2018) with Tamra Stambaugh. She recently coedited a special issue of *Gifted Child Quarterly* with Tamra Stambaugh on the topic of poverty. She has received numerous awards for her work, including the Ann F. Isaacs Founder's Award from NAGC in 2017 for contributions to the field of gifted education. Earlier awards include the Distinguished Scholar Award, the Distinguished Achievement Award, the Early Leader Award, and the Legacy Award from NAGC. She also received awards from the higher education community, including the State Council of Higher Education and the Alpha Chapter of Phi Beta Kappa, for her accomplishments. Mensa has also awarded her its Lifetime Achievement Award, as did her alma mater, The University of Toledo.